Table of Contents

Introduction 5
The Mystery Behind Valentine's Day 5
A Glimpse into Ancient Love Traditions 9
Evolution of Love Celebrations through the Ages 13
Chapter 1: Love in Ancient Rome 18
Feast of Lupercalia: Fertility and Romance 18
Roman Gods of Love: Cupid and Venus 21
Romantic Legends: Mark Antony and Cleopatra 26
Romantic Rituals and Traditions 30
Chapter 2: Christian Influence on Love Celebrations 35
St. Valentine: The Patron Saint of Love 35
Christianizing Roman Festivals 41
Chaucer and the Birth of Valentine's Day Poetry 47
Valentine's Day as a Day of Courtly Love 53
Chapter 3: Valentine's Day in the Renaissance 58
The Rise of Valentine's Day Cards 58
Literary Contributions to Valentine's Day 64
Queen Victoria and the Romantic Revival 68
Valentine's Day Traditions in the 18th and 19th Centuries 73
Chapter 4: Commercialization and Modernization ... 78
The Industrial Revolution and Mass Production of Valentine's Cards 78
Emergence of the Floral Industry on Valentine's Day 83
Candy, Chocolates, and Valentine's Day 90
Valentine's Day in the 20th Century 96
Chapter 5: Globalization of Love Celebrations 102
Valentine's Day Around the World 102
Cultural Adaptations and Traditions 108
Global Icons of Love and Romance 114

Controversies and Criticisms Worldwide *120*
Chapter 6: Contemporary Expressions of Love 125
Technological Influences on Modern Romance *125*
Changing Dynamics of Romantic Relationships *131*
Celebrity Influence on Valentine's Day Trends *137*
Virtual Celebrations and Long-Distance Love *142*
Chapter 7: The Science of Love................................. 147
The Psychology of Love *147*
Biological Basis of Romance *155*
Love and the Brain: A Scientific Perspective *163*
Cultural and Societal Influences on Love *171*
Conclusion: Love Across Time and Borders 178
The Everlasting Symbolism of Love *178*
Legacy of Valentine's Day Traditions *183*
Looking Forward: Love in the Future *189*
Glossary.. 195
Potential References 198

Copyright © 2024 by Blaze X. Maverick (Author)

All rights reserved. This book or any portion thereof may not be reproduced or used in any manner whatsoever without the express written permission of the publisher except for the use of brief quotations in a book review.

This book is copyright protected. This is only for personal use. You cannot amend, distributor, sell, use, quote or paraphrase any part or the content within this book without the consent of the author.

Please note the information contained within this document is for educational and entertainment purposes only. Every attempt has been made to provide accurate, up to date and reliable complete information. No warranties of any kind are expressed or implied. Readers acknowledge that the author is not engaging in the rendering of legal, financial, medical or professional advice. The content of this book has been derived from various sources. Please consult a licensed professional before attempting any techniques outlined in this book.

By reading this document, the readers agree that under no circumstances are the author responsible for any losses, direct or indirect, which are incurred as a result of the use of information contained within this document, including but not limited to errors, omissions or inaccuracies.

Thank you very much for reading this book.

Title: Unveiling the Heart of Valentine's Day
Subtitle: A Glimpse into Ancient Love Traditions

Series: Eternal Valentine: Stories of Enduring Love: From Ancient Traditions to Modern Expressions
Author: Blaze X. Maverick

Introduction
The Mystery Behind Valentine's Day

As we delve into the enchanting tapestry of Valentine's Day, a celebration revered globally as a day of love and affection, we find ourselves standing at the intersection of history, mythology, and timeless romance. The origins of this cherished day are veiled in mystery, obscured by the passage of centuries and the amalgamation of diverse cultural influences. In this section, we embark on a journey to unravel the enigma that shrouds the genesis of Valentine's Day, exploring the various narratives and historical tendrils that have contributed to its rich tapestry.

Love's Ancient Roots: An Ambiguous Beginning

Valentine's Day, with its roots stretching far back into the annals of time, emerges as a celebration that defies a singular origin. The threads of its inception intertwine with ancient Roman fertility festivals, Christian martyrs, and poetic musings from medieval Europe. The journey begins with the Feast of Lupercalia, a Roman festival brimming with fertility rites and romantic rituals. Here, love was entwined with the whims of Cupid and the grace of Venus, setting the stage for the romantic traditions that would follow.

Saint Valentine: A Martyr's Legacy

The mystique of Valentine's Day gains resonance with the emergence of Saint Valentine, a figure enshrouded in historical ambiguity. Various legends and accounts claim the existence of multiple individuals named Valentine, all martyrs who met their fate in different ways. The convergence of these narratives weaves a tapestry of devotion, courage, and the enduring spirit of love. From clandestine marriages to acts of compassion, Saint Valentine's legacy becomes the cornerstone of the modern celebration.

Chaucer's Influence: A Flourish of Poetry

The transition from antiquity to the medieval era introduces Geoffrey Chaucer and his seminal work, "The Parliament of Fowls." Chaucer's poetic prowess breathed new life into Valentine's Day, elevating it from a historical commemoration to a day of courtly love. The verses penned by Chaucer intricately wove the notions of romantic love into the fabric of Valentine's Day, forever altering its trajectory and setting the stage for the romantic expressions that would follow.

Renaissance Reverie: Love Blossoms Anew

As we step into the Renaissance, we witness the blossoming of love in myriad forms. The era witnesses the rise of Valentine's Day cards, crafted with meticulous artistry and exchanged as tokens of affection. The literary luminaries of the time, from Shakespeare to Donne, contribute to the romantic fervor surrounding the day. Queen Victoria herself plays a role in the romantic revival, solidifying Valentine's Day as a cherished tradition in the 18th and 19th centuries.

Commercialization and the 20th Century: A Love Story Unfolds

The 20th century ushers in an era of mass production, industrialization, and the commercialization of love. The emergence of the floral and confectionery industries transforms Valentine's Day into a consumer-driven celebration. Greeting cards, adorned with intricate designs and sentimental verses, become a ubiquitous expression of love. As we navigate through the evolution of the day, we witness the intersection of tradition and commerce, forever altering the landscape of Valentine's Day.

Globalization: Love Knows No Borders

The globalization of love celebrations takes center stage as we traverse diverse cultures and traditions. From Asia to Africa, from Europe to the Americas, the universal language of love adapts to local customs and rituals. Yet, as the celebration expands its reach, controversies and criticisms emerge. Cultural clashes and debates surrounding the authenticity of love on a prescribed day underscore the complexities woven into the global fabric of Valentine's Day.

Contemporary Expressions: Love in a Digital Age

The 21st century unfolds with unprecedented technological advancements, reshaping the dynamics of modern romance. Social media, dating apps, and virtual connections redefine how love is expressed and experienced. Celebrities become influencers, shaping trends and influencing expressions of love. Virtual celebrations and long-distance relationships take center stage, offering new dimensions to the age-old celebration.

The Science of Love: Decoding Matters of the Heart

As we seek to demystify the profound emotions associated with Valentine's Day, we delve into the scientific underpinnings of love. The psychology of love, the biological basis of romance, and the intricate dance between brain chemistry and emotion unveil the intricate tapestry that forms the essence of human connection. Cultural and societal influences further shape our understanding of love, casting light on the multifaceted nature of this timeless emotion.

Love Across Time and Borders: An Enduring Legacy

In our exploration of the heart of Valentine's Day, we find ourselves at the crossroads of past, present, and future. The legacy of Valentine's Day traditions, shaped by centuries of cultural, religious, and societal influences, stands as a testament to the enduring power of love. As we gaze into the future, we contemplate the evolving nature of love and the ever-changing expressions of affection that will define Valentine's Day for generations to come.

A Glimpse into Ancient Love Traditions

In the vast tapestry of time, where threads of history weave a narrative of love and affection, ancient civilizations stand as pioneers, laying the foundations for the celebration we now know as Valentine's Day. As we delve into the enigmatic origins of love traditions that have transcended centuries, we unearth the fascinating customs and rituals of ancient cultures that contributed to the evolution of this cherished day.

The Cradle of Love: Mesopotamia and Egypt

Our journey into ancient love traditions commences in the cradle of civilization, Mesopotamia. Here, in the fertile lands between the Tigris and Euphrates rivers, love was intertwined with the divine. The goddess Inanna, presiding over love and fertility, was venerated through rituals and celebrations that sought to invoke the blessings of passion and procreation. Love, in its raw and primal form, was a force acknowledged and revered.

Moving southward to the banks of the Nile, ancient Egypt unfolds as a realm where love was immortalized in hieroglyphs and tombs. The concept of eternal love, symbolized by the union of Osiris and Isis, permeated Egyptian society. Intricate love poems adorned papyrus scrolls, capturing the essence of romantic yearning and desire. The Nile, with its life-giving waters, mirrored the cyclical nature of love and regeneration.

The Eternal Flame of Greece

In the radiant glow of ancient Greece, love took on a multifaceted brilliance, personified by the Greek gods and goddesses. Eros, the mischievous god of love, wielded his arrows capriciously, igniting the flames of desire in mortal hearts. The Greek symposiums, gatherings where intellect and emotion converged, became stages for expressions of love and admiration.

The epic poetry of Homer, encapsulated in works like the Iliad and the Odyssey, showcased the complexities of love amidst the backdrop of heroic endeavors. In the dialogue of Plato, the philosophical underpinnings of love were explored, presenting love as an ethereal force that transcended physicality. Ancient Greece, with its celebration of beauty, intellect, and the human spirit, bestowed upon us a legacy of love that resonates through the corridors of time.

Rome: Love in the Shadows of Empire

As we traverse the expansive reaches of the Roman Empire, we encounter a civilization where love unfolded against the grandeur of conquest and imperial splendor. The festival of Lupercalia, an ancient Roman celebration held in mid-February, marked a juncture where fertility and love converged. The rituals involved the sacrifice of goats and the symbolic purification of the city, believed to ensure health and fertility.

Within the pantheon of Roman deities, Cupid and Venus emerged as the guardians of love. Cupid, armed with his bow and arrow, became an enduring symbol of romantic attraction. Venus, the goddess of love and beauty, presided over matters of the heart. The romantic legends of Mark Antony and Cleopatra added a touch of passion and tragedy, immortalizing love in the annals of history.

China: The Red Thread of Fate

Far to the east, in ancient China, love was entwined with the concept of destiny. The legend of the Red Thread, a mythical cord believed to connect those destined to be soulmates, captured the imagination of the Chinese people.

Love, in this ancient realm, transcended time and space, guided by an invisible force that bound hearts together.

Chinese poetry, with its delicate verses and profound expressions, became a vehicle for conveying the nuances of love. The peony, a symbol of love and prosperity, adorned the gardens as a testament to the enduring nature of romantic connections. Ancient China gifted the world a poetic and philosophical perspective on love, where the threads of fate intricately wove the stories of lovers.

India: The Dance of Radha and Krishna

In the vibrant tapestry of ancient India, love found expression in the tales of gods and goddesses, particularly in the divine romance of Radha and Krishna. The pastoral setting of Vrindavan became a backdrop for the playful and enchanting love between Krishna, the divine cowherd, and Radha, his beloved consort. Their love transcended societal norms, symbolizing the union of the individual soul with the divine.

The ancient Indian treatise, the Kama Sutra, offered a comprehensive exploration of love, encompassing both physical and emotional dimensions. Love, in ancient India, was viewed as a sacred and transformative force that permeated every aspect of life. The poetry of Kalidasa and other ancient Indian poets celebrated the beauty of love in verses that echoed through the ages.

Persia: The Garden of Roses

Journeying into ancient Persia, we discover a realm where love was likened to a blossoming garden of roses. The Persian poets, notably Rumi, crafted verses that spoke of the intoxicating fragrance of love and the ecstatic dance of the soul. The metaphor of the rose, with its thorns and petals, became a symbol of the complexities inherent in matters of the heart.

The celebration of Nowruz, the Persian New Year, marked a time of renewal and the blossoming of nature—a fitting backdrop for expressions of love. The concept of "ishq," a profound and selfless love, permeated Persian culture, leaving an indelible mark on the poetic landscape of the region. Ancient Persia gifted the world a poetic ode to the transformative power of love.

Love Across Cultures: A Harmonious Melody

As we reflect on these glimpses into ancient love traditions, a harmonious melody emerges—a universal language spoken by civilizations separated by time and space. From the banks of the Tigris to the gardens of Vrindavan, love unfolded as a force that transcended cultural boundaries, leaving an indelible imprint on the collective consciousness of humanity.

In the subsequent chapters, we will trace the evolution of these ancient love traditions, examining how they merged, diverged, and ultimately contributed to the rich mosaic that is Valentine's Day. The threads of love, intricately woven by ancient civilizations, continue to bind us to the timeless celebration of affection and connection.

Evolution of Love Celebrations through the Ages

As we stand on the precipice of time, gazing into the intricate tapestry of human history, the celebration of love emerges as a constant thread woven through the ages. From ancient rituals to modern-day expressions, the evolution of love celebrations is a compelling journey marked by cultural shifts, societal changes, and the enduring human quest for connection. In this exploration, we unravel the layers of time, tracing the metamorphosis of love celebrations from their nascent origins to the multifaceted celebration we recognize as Valentine's Day today.

Love's Antiquity: From Fertility Festivals to Sacred Unions

The roots of love celebrations extend deep into antiquity, where the primal forces of nature were intimately entwined with human existence. Fertility festivals, such as the Feast of Lupercalia in ancient Rome, marked a juncture where love, fertility, and purification converged. Rituals involving sacrifices, symbolic cleansings, and the drawing of lots sought to invoke divine blessings for the prosperity of the community.

In ancient Mesopotamia and Egypt, love found expression in the veneration of deities associated with fertility and passion. The divine unions of gods and goddesses mirrored the earthly aspirations for enduring love. These early celebrations set the stage for a cultural landscape where love was both a natural force and a divine blessing.

Christianity's Embrace: From Martyrs to Courtly Love

The advent of Christianity ushered in a new chapter in the evolution of love celebrations. The Christianization of Roman festivals, including Lupercalia, aimed to redirect the focus from pagan rituals to the veneration of Christian saints.

Among these saints, St. Valentine emerged as a figure whose legacy became synonymous with love and devotion.

The intertwining of Christian traditions with existing celebrations laid the groundwork for the emergence of Valentine's Day. Chaucer, with his poetic musings, elevated the day to a celebration of courtly love—a refined and idealized form of romantic expression. Love, once entangled with fertility rites, now bore the influence of Christian virtues and the delicate dance of courtship.

Renaissance Romance: From Cards to Literary Contributions

As society transitioned into the Renaissance, expressions of love took on new dimensions. The exchange of love letters and tokens became a popular practice, setting the stage for the eventual rise of Valentine's Day cards. The artistic and literary contributions of the era, from Shakespearean sonnets to elaborate love letters, added layers of sophistication to the celebration of love.

The tradition of sending handwritten notes expressing affection became a hallmark of Valentine's Day. The crafting of ornate cards adorned with lace, ribbons, and sentimental verses became an art form. The literary luminaries of the time, including Shakespeare and Donne, immortalized the complexities of love in works that resonated with the passions of the Renaissance.

Commercialization and the Industrial Revolution: Love in Mass Production

The Industrial Revolution marked a turning point in the evolution of love celebrations. With advancements in printing technology, the mass production of Valentine's Day cards became possible. The intricate craftsmanship of handmade cards gave way to the accessibility of pre-designed cards, allowing for a broader and more democratized expression of affection.

The emergence of the floral industry as a symbol of love added a visual and aromatic dimension to Valentine's Day. Roses, with their timeless association with love, became the quintessential floral expression. The exchange of chocolates, another industry born in this era, further solidified the commercialization of love celebrations. The commodification of love, while criticized by some, opened new avenues for expressing sentiments on a grand scale.

Globalization of Love: Cultural Adaptations and Controversies

As the world entered the 20th century, love celebrations transcended geographical boundaries. Valentine's Day, once rooted in Western traditions, began to spread globally, adapting to the diverse cultures it touched. While the celebration resonated with many, it also encountered resistance and controversies in different parts of the world.

Cultural adaptations ranged from unique customs in Japan, where women traditionally present gifts to men, to the celebration of Friendship Day in Latin American countries. Yet, as the celebration expanded its reach, cultural clashes emerged. Some questioned the authenticity of love on a prescribed day, while others grappled with the intrusion of Western values into local traditions. Valentine's Day became a global phenomenon, both celebrated and scrutinized for its impact on cultural identity.

Contemporary Expressions: Love in a Digital Age

In the 21st century, the evolution of love celebrations underwent a paradigm shift with the advent of technology. The digital age transformed how love is expressed, experienced, and shared. Social media platforms became virtual canvases for declarations of love, relationship statuses, and the sharing of romantic milestones.

The rise of dating apps altered the dynamics of modern romance, providing new avenues for people to connect across distances. Celebrity influencers played a pivotal role in shaping trends and influencing expressions of love. Virtual celebrations and long-distance relationships became commonplace, reflecting the changing landscape of human connections in an interconnected world.

The Science of Love: Exploring Matters of the Heart

Beyond the realms of tradition and technology, the evolution of love celebrations extends into the scientific understanding of human emotions. Psychologists delve into the intricacies of love, examining the various forms it takes and the psychological underpinnings that govern human connections. The biological basis of romance, including the role of hormones and neurotransmitters, adds a layer of complexity to the age-old phenomenon of love.

Neuroscience explores the brain's response to love, unraveling the intricate dance between emotion and cognition. Cultural and societal influences, from family structures to societal norms, shape the ways in which love is perceived and expressed. The science of love provides a lens through which we can comprehend the profound and often mysterious nature of this universal experience.

Love Across Time and Borders: A Tapestry Unfolding

As we reflect on the evolution of love celebrations through the ages, we find ourselves at the intersection of tradition and innovation, history and progress. The celebration of love, from its primal origins to its contemporary expressions, stands as a testament to the enduring human need for connection and intimacy.

In the subsequent chapters, we will continue our exploration, delving into the cultural nuances, global adaptations, and scientific insights that have shaped the celebration of love. From ancient rituals to modern-day digital expressions, the evolution of love celebrations unfolds as a dynamic tapestry, weaving together the diverse threads of human experience.

Chapter 1: Love in Ancient Rome
Feast of Lupercalia: Fertility and Romance

In the heart of ancient Rome, amidst the grandeur of the Republic, love found itself intertwined with a celebration both primal and enchanting—the Feast of Lupercalia. This annual festival, observed from the 13th to the 15th of February, marked a juncture where fertility, purification, and romantic inclinations converged in a tapestry of rituals that would later influence the trajectory of Valentine's Day.

Origins in Ancient Rites: A Celebration of Wolves and Fertility

The origins of Lupercalia are rooted in ancient Roman mythology, reaching back to a time when the city's destiny was still unfolding. Legend has it that the festival traces its roots to the she-wolf who nursed the abandoned twins, Romulus and Remus, the legendary founders of Rome. The Lupercal, the cave where the she-wolf was believed to have sheltered the twins, became the sacred site from which the festival derived its name.

The Lupercalia rituals were overseen by a group of priests known as the Luperci, who traced their lineage to the earliest days of Rome. Clad in goatskins, symbolizing the pastoral origins of the festival, the Luperci embarked on a series of ceremonies aimed at invoking the blessings of fertility and warding off malevolent forces.

Purification through Sacrifice: The Rituals of the Luperci

The heart of Lupercalia lay in its purification rituals, performed with a fervor that mirrored the primal instincts of early Roman society. The Luperci would gather at the sacred cave and offer sacrifices, usually goats and a dog, symbolizing fertility and the untamed forces of nature. The ritualistic slaying of these animals was believed to purify the city and ensure the prosperity of its inhabitants.

Following the sacrifice, the priests would strip the goatskins from the sacrificial animals and fashion them into thongs, known as "februa." Armed with these symbolic instruments, the Luperci would then proceed to the streets of Rome, where crowds eagerly awaited their purifying touch.

The Fertility Run: A Lively Spectacle of Tradition

The highlight of Lupercalia was the fertility run, a lively and boisterous spectacle that unfolded through the streets of Rome. As the Luperci, clad in goatskins and wielding the februa, traversed the city, they would playfully strike those who crossed their path. Far from being a punitive gesture, these ritualistic strikes were believed to bestow fertility and blessings upon those touched.

Women, in particular, eagerly awaited the passage of the Luperci, often baring their skin to receive the symbolic lashings. It was widely believed that being touched by the februa would increase a woman's chances of conceiving and ensure a smooth and prosperous childbirth. The festivities reached a crescendo as the city resonated with laughter, shouts, and the rhythmic drumming of hooves—the lively spirit of Lupercalia permeating every corner of Rome.

Cupid's Arrow and the Role of Eros: Romance in Lupercalia

While Lupercalia was undeniably a festival rooted in fertility and purification, it also held a romantic undercurrent that would later influence the imagery of Valentine's Day. The association with Cupid, the mischievous god of love, added a layer of enchantment to the festivities. Cupid, often depicted with his bow and arrow, was believed to be present during Lupercalia, guiding the hearts of those touched by the februa.

The symbolism of Cupid's arrow, representing the sudden and unpredictable nature of love, became intertwined with the festival. The notion that love could strike unexpectedly, much like the playful lashings of the Luperci, added a whimsical and romantic element to the celebrations. The intertwining of fertility and love during Lupercalia set the stage for the evolution of romantic traditions in ancient Rome.

Legacy and Influence: From Lupercalia to Valentine's Day

As the Roman Empire expanded and underwent cultural transformations, the traditions of Lupercalia persisted, albeit with modifications. The Christianization of Rome sought to align the festival with Christian values, leading to the eventual assimilation of Lupercalia into the emerging celebration of St. Valentine's Day.

The echoes of Lupercalia resonate in the modern imagery of Valentine's Day—the playful exchange of tokens of affection, the symbolic gestures of love, and the association with Cupid's arrows. While the explicit fertility rituals have faded into history, the spirit of Lupercalia continues to permeate the celebration of love, serving as a bridge between the ancient past and the contemporary expressions of affection.

In the subsequent chapters, we will further explore the influence of Roman gods of love, romantic legends, and the evolution of love traditions in ancient Rome. The Feast of Lupercalia, with its primal energy and romantic undertones, stands as a testament to the enduring power of love celebrations through the ages.

Roman Gods of Love: Cupid and Venus

In the heart of ancient Rome, where mythology and daily life intertwined, the gods held sway over every aspect of existence. Love, being a fundamental and transcendent force, found its divine representation in the captivating figures of Cupid and Venus. As we explore the mythic realm of these gods, we uncover the intricate stories that shaped the Roman understanding of love, desire, and the eternal dance between mortal hearts.

Cupid: The Mischievous Archer of Love

At the forefront of Roman love mythology stands Cupid, a mischievous and capricious deity whose arrows could pierce the hearts of gods and mortals alike. The Roman adaptation of the Greek god Eros, Cupid was not merely a cherubic symbol of love but a formidable force capable of inspiring passion, desire, and sometimes, chaos.

Depicted as a winged youth armed with a bow and arrows, Cupid embodied the unpredictable nature of love. His arrows, tipped with enchantment, had the power to incite love and desire in those they struck. The dichotomy of Cupid, with his innocent appearance juxtaposed with his potent influence, became a central theme in Roman art, literature, and folklore.

The Birth of Cupid: Myths and Symbolism

The myth of Cupid's birth is woven with layers of symbolism and drama. According to Roman mythology, Cupid was the son of Venus, the goddess of love and beauty. His father, however, remained a subject of debate among ancient writers. Some narratives attribute Cupid's paternity to Mars, the god of war, while others propose Mercury, the messenger god, as his divine father.

One of the most iconic tales of Cupid's origin involves his mother, Venus, and her desire to make the god of war more approachable. In this narrative, Cupid's mischievous nature is evident from the beginning. His birth, whether from the union of Venus and Mars or another divine liaison, encapsulates the unpredictable and sometimes tumultuous nature of love itself.

Cupid's Pranks: Love Unleashed

The stories of Cupid's exploits are rife with whimsical pranks and amorous adventures. His playful nature often led him to target both gods and mortals with his enchanted arrows, sparking love and desire where they least expected it. From causing gods to fall in love with mortals to inciting romantic entanglements among unsuspecting couples, Cupid's interventions were both entertaining and unpredictable.

One of the most famous tales involves Cupid's encounter with the mortal Psyche. Ordered by his mother Venus to make Psyche fall in love with a monstrous creature, Cupid himself becomes enamored with her beauty. The ensuing narrative unfolds as a testament to the transformative power of love, with trials, tribulations, and a union that defies both mortal and divine expectations.

Venus: Goddess of Love and Beauty

If Cupid personified the unpredictable and impulsive nature of love, Venus, his mother, embodied the timeless elegance and allure of romantic attraction. As the goddess of love, beauty, and fertility, Venus held a revered position in the Roman pantheon, and her influence extended far beyond matters of the heart.

Often depicted as a radiant and ethereal figure, Venus commanded adoration from gods and mortals alike. Her association with love went beyond the romantic; it encompassed the full spectrum of human connections, from familial bonds to the unity of communities. Temples dedicated to Venus dotted the Roman landscape, underscoring the integral role she played in the daily lives of the people.

Venus's Origins: Birth from Sea Foam

The myth of Venus's birth is a tale of divine beauty and celestial origins. According to one prominent narrative, Venus emerged from the sea foam after the castration of Uranus, the primal god of the sky, by his son Cronus. As Uranus's blood mingled with the sea, Venus arose, a symbol of beauty and renewal.

The famous painting by Sandro Botticelli, "The Birth of Venus," captures the essence of this myth, depicting the goddess standing on a seashell, surrounded by nymphs and zephyrs. The image immortalizes Venus's connection to the sea and her emergence as the epitome of love and beauty.

Venus and Mars: A Divine Union

The tales of Venus's romantic entanglements were not limited to her relationship with Cupid. One of the most notable liaisons involved Mars, the god of war. The union of Venus and Mars symbolized the harmonious balance between love and conflict, passion and strife. While Mars embodied the raw and masculine aspects of power, Venus brought forth the softer and nurturing qualities of love.

Their union was believed to be the genesis of several divine offspring, including Cupid, further intertwining the divine lineage of love within the Roman pantheon. The connection between Venus and Mars became a recurring theme in art, literature, and mythology, illustrating the delicate interplay between the forces of love and war.

Cult of Venus: Worship and Festivals

The worship of Venus permeated Roman society, and numerous temples were dedicated to her throughout the empire. The most renowned among these was the Temple of Venus Genetrix in Rome, commissioned by Julius Caesar to honor Venus as the divine mother of the Roman people. The cult of Venus Genetrix celebrated the goddess's role in the creation and preservation of the Roman state.

Festivals dedicated to Venus, such as the Veneralia, were observed with reverence and enthusiasm. These celebrations involved rituals, offerings, and processions, all aimed at invoking Venus's blessings and ensuring the prosperity of love in all its forms. The cult of Venus served as a unifying force, emphasizing the interconnectedness of romantic love, familial bonds, and the well-being of the state.

Venus in Art and Literature: A Muse for Creativity

The enduring influence of Venus extended into the realms of art and literature, where her image and mythology inspired countless masterpieces. Artists sought to capture the idealized beauty and grace associated with Venus, portraying her in various poses and settings. From the delicate sculptures of Praxiteles to the Renaissance paintings of Botticelli and Titian, Venus became a muse for creativity and a symbol of transcendent beauty.

In literature, Venus's presence permeated works such as Ovid's "Metamorphoses" and Virgil's "Aeneid." Her influence in these texts transcended mere romantic entanglements, weaving into the broader narrative of creation, transformation, and the interconnectedness of divine and mortal destinies.

Legacy of Cupid and Venus: Love in the Roman Imagination

The legacy of Cupid and Venus reverberates through the corridors of Roman history, leaving an indelible mark on the collective imagination of the empire. Their stories, depicted in art, celebrated in festivals, and woven into the fabric of daily life, served as a cultural touchstone for understanding the complexities and nuances of love.

As we continue our exploration of love in ancient Rome, we will delve deeper into the romantic legends, rituals, and traditions that shaped the celebration of love. Cupid and Venus, with their mythical allure and divine influence, stand as eternal symbols of the enduring power of love in all its forms.

Romantic Legends: Mark Antony and Cleopatra

In the annals of ancient history, few love stories evoke the passion, drama, and tragedy as that of Mark Antony and Cleopatra. Their union, entwined with political intrigue, opulence, and undying devotion, stands as a testament to the intertwining of love and power in the ancient world. As we navigate the labyrinth of their romantic saga, the tale of Mark Antony and Cleopatra emerges as a chapter of love that transcended borders, defied conventions, and ultimately became immortalized in the pages of history.

The Stage Set: A World in Turmoil

The backdrop for the love story of Mark Antony and Cleopatra is the turbulent canvas of the Roman Republic in the 1st century BCE. Mark Antony, a formidable Roman general and statesman, found himself thrust into the political turmoil that followed the assassination of Julius Caesar in 44 BCE. As a member of the Second Triumvirate, Antony wielded considerable power alongside Octavian (later known as Augustus) and Lepidus.

In the eastern reaches of the Roman Empire, Cleopatra, the last pharaoh of Egypt, presided over a kingdom that had thrived for centuries. Cleopatra's intelligence, charm, and political acumen made her a figure of fascination and power. The meeting of Mark Antony and Cleopatra would set the stage for a love story that would echo through the corridors of time.

Meeting of Hearts: The Union of Mark Antony and Cleopatra

The initial encounter between Mark Antony and Cleopatra unfolded against the opulent backdrop of Cleopatra's palace in Alexandria. The queen, known for her charisma and allure, set out to seduce the Roman general, both politically and romantically. Cleopatra, aware of the intricate dance of power in the Roman world, saw in Antony an opportunity to secure the safety and autonomy of Egypt.

The first meeting, often described as a calculated and sumptuous affair, laid the foundation for a connection that would transcend political alliances. Cleopatra's ability to captivate Mark Antony was not merely a result of physical attraction but a manifestation of her intellect, wit, and the exotic charm of Egypt itself. The love that blossomed between them would become a force that defied conventions and navigated the treacherous currents of Roman politics.

The Alexandrian Court: Love Amidst Luxury

The union of Mark Antony and Cleopatra unfolded amidst the splendors of Cleopatra's court in Alexandria. The queen, renowned for her lavish lifestyle and patronage of the arts, created an environment of luxury and indulgence. Banquets, performances, and grand processions celebrated the opulence of Egypt, providing a rich backdrop for the romance between the Roman general and the Egyptian queen.

The couple's public displays of affection and shared moments of revelry became legendary. Cleopatra, in her efforts to align herself with the divine, often portrayed herself as the goddess Isis, emphasizing the mystical and otherworldly dimensions of their union. The lavishness of their courtship fueled both admiration and condemnation, depending on the perspective of those observing this unconventional love affair.

Struggles for Power: The Political Landscape

The love between Mark Antony and Cleopatra, while profound, was not immune to the political currents of the time. In Rome, the alliance between Antony and Cleopatra stirred suspicion and animosity among political rivals, particularly

Octavian. The political ramifications of Antony's association with the Egyptian queen became a rallying point for those who sought to undermine his influence in Rome.

The situation escalated as Antony and Cleopatra formed both personal and political alliances. The Donations of Alexandria, a grand ceremony in which Antony recognized the children he had with Cleopatra as legitimate heirs to various territories, further fueled the ire of those who perceived this as a threat to Roman power dynamics. The love between Antony and Cleopatra became entangled with the complex web of Roman politics, leading to a series of events that would alter the course of history.

The Tragedy of Actium: Love Amidst War

The turning point in the saga of Mark Antony and Cleopatra came on the fields of Actium in 31 BCE. The naval battle between the forces of Octavian and Antony marked the culmination of simmering tensions and political rivalries. The love affair between the Roman general and the Egyptian queen was now played out on the stage of war, and the outcome would seal their fate.

As the forces of Octavian gained the upper hand, Cleopatra's fleet retreated, and Antony, believing falsely that Cleopatra had perished, took his own life. The tragedy of Actium bore witness to the sacrifice of love in the face of political turmoil. Cleopatra, upon learning of Antony's death, took refuge in her mausoleum, where she would join him in death rather than be paraded through the streets of Rome as a captive.

Legacy of Love and Tragedy: Immortalized in History

The love story of Mark Antony and Cleopatra, marked by passion, politics, and ultimate tragedy, left an indelible mark on the annals of history. The couple's deaths marked the end of the Ptolemaic Kingdom and the beginning of Egypt as a Roman province. Their story became a symbol of love's ability to transcend boundaries but also a cautionary tale of the interplay between personal desires and political consequences.

The dramatic narrative of Mark Antony and Cleopatra found resonance in subsequent artistic, literary, and theatrical works. William Shakespeare immortalized their love in his play "Antony and Cleopatra," capturing the grandeur and tragedy of their romance. Artists through the ages, from ancient frescoes to modern canvases, sought to portray the allure and complexity of this iconic couple.

Conclusion: Love and Destiny

The love story of Mark Antony and Cleopatra, though shrouded in the mists of time, continues to captivate the imagination. It serves as a poignant reminder of the enduring interplay between love and destiny, passion and politics. In the subsequent chapters, we will delve into the broader landscape of love in ancient Rome, exploring the romantic traditions, rituals, and cultural nuances that shaped the celebration of love in this fascinating era. Mark Antony and Cleopatra, with their timeless saga, beckon us to ponder the profound mysteries of love, destiny, and the indomitable spirit of the human heart.

Romantic Rituals and Traditions

In the tapestry of ancient Rome, love was not only an abstract concept but a lived experience woven into the fabric of daily life. The Romans, known for their elaborate customs and traditions, had a multifaceted approach to expressing and celebrating love. From courtship rituals to marriage ceremonies, the romantic landscape of ancient Rome was rich with symbolism, tradition, and a deep connection to both the divine and the earthly realms.

Courtship in Ancient Rome: The Dance of Hearts

The journey of love in ancient Rome often began with courtship, a delicate dance of hearts where the rituals were both nuanced and symbolic. While marriages were sometimes arranged for political or economic reasons, the concept of mutual affection and compatibility played a crucial role in courtship.

Flirtation and subtle gestures marked the initial stages of courtship. A meaningful glance, a shared smile, or the exchange of small tokens became the language of love. Gifts, such as jewelry or poetry, were often exchanged as expressions of affection. In a society where the sanctity of the family unit was paramount, the process of courtship was not only a personal matter but one that carried societal implications.

The Role of Betrothal: Promises and Contracts

Betrothal, a formal agreement to marry, played a pivotal role in the progression of romantic relationships in ancient Rome. While the concept of betrothal might evoke images of arranged marriages, it encompassed a broader range of unions. Betrothal involved the exchange of vows and promises, creating a binding commitment that laid the foundation for the future marriage.

The exchange of engagement rings, often made of iron or gold, symbolized the enduring nature of the betrothal. These rings, sometimes adorned with intricate engravings or inscriptions, served as tangible reminders of the promises made between the betrothed couple. The formalization of the betrothal carried legal weight, and breaking such an agreement could lead to legal consequences.

The Ceremony of Conubium: Uniting Hearts in Marriage

The pinnacle of love and commitment in ancient Rome was the sacred institution of marriage, symbolized by the ceremony of conubium. The Romans held marriage in high regard, viewing it as a fundamental building block of society. The ceremony involved a series of rituals and traditions that sanctified the union between a man and a woman.

The exchange of vows, known as "nuptiae," formed the heart of the marriage ceremony. The couple, dressed in special attire, would declare their commitment to each other before witnesses and, often, a priest. The words spoken during the nuptiae carried significant legal and religious weight, binding the couple in a sacred covenant.

The Importance of Festivities: Celebrating Unions

Marriage ceremonies were not merely solemn affairs but joyful celebrations that extended beyond the couple to their families and the community. Festivities, including feasts, music, and dancing, marked the joyous occasion of a wedding. The communal nature of these celebrations reflected the belief that marriage was not only a union of two individuals but a joining of families and, by extension, a reinforcement of social bonds.

The Romans believed in the auspicious nature of certain dates for weddings, with June being considered particularly favorable. The concept of the "June bride" has its roots in Roman traditions, where the goddess Juno, protector of marriage and women, was honored during this month. Couples sought the blessings of Juno for a prosperous and fertile union.

Symbols of Union: The Matrimonial Bed and the Knot of Hercules

Central to the rituals of marriage in ancient Rome was the symbolism associated with the matrimonial bed. The act of carrying the bride over the threshold of her new home symbolized her transition from the protection of her father to the care of her husband. The bed itself, adorned with flowers and garlands, represented fertility and the hope for a fruitful union.

The Knot of Hercules, also known as the "nodus Herculanus," was a ceremonial knot tied around the bride's waist during the wedding ceremony. This intricate knot, symbolizing the bonds of marriage, was believed to be difficult to untie, signifying the enduring nature of the marital commitment. The symbolism of the knot extended to the idea that the marriage should be as challenging to unravel as untying the complex Hercules knot.

Love Tokens and Offerings: Expressions of Devotion

Expressions of love in ancient Rome extended beyond the rituals of courtship and marriage to encompass ongoing gestures of affection within marital unions. Love tokens, often exchanged between spouses, took various forms. Jewelry, engraved with expressions of love or symbolic motifs, served as tangible reminders of the emotional connection between partners.

Offerings to deities associated with love and marriage were also common. Couples might make offerings at temples dedicated to Juno, Venus, or other gods and goddesses believed to oversee marital bonds. The act of seeking divine favor through offerings reflected the Roman belief in the importance of the gods' blessings for the success and longevity of a marriage.

The Concept of Pietas: Devotion in Relationships

The Roman concept of "pietas," often translated as devotion or filial duty, extended to romantic relationships. Pietas represented a sense of duty, loyalty, and reverence within familial and societal bonds. In the context of love, pietas emphasized the importance of mutual respect, faithfulness, and commitment between partners.

The ideal Roman marriage was one characterized by pietas, where both spouses upheld their responsibilities and maintained a harmonious household. The principles of pietas extended to the broader familial context, emphasizing the interconnectedness of family relationships and the importance of maintaining societal order through virtuous conduct.

The Role of Divorce: Legal Dissolution of Unions

While the Romans held marriage in high regard, they recognized that not all unions stood the test of time. Divorce, though not as common as in contemporary times, was a legal and socially accepted process. A divorce, known as "divortium," could be initiated by either party, and valid reasons included issues such as infertility, adultery, or irreconcilable differences.

The legal formalities of divorce involved the couple appearing before a magistrate, with the process often requiring the return of the dowry and the division of shared property. Despite the ease with which a divorce could be obtained, societal norms encouraged couples to resolve their differences and maintain the sanctity of the marital bond.

Conclusion: Love's Enduring Legacy

In the mosaic of romantic rituals and traditions in ancient Rome, the themes of commitment, symbolism, and societal bonds were intricately woven. Love, viewed through the lens of courtship, marriage, and ongoing devotion, became a foundational element in the societal fabric. The rituals and traditions surrounding love in ancient Rome not only reflected the values of the time but also laid the groundwork for the enduring legacy of love that transcends the boundaries of culture and time. In the subsequent chapters, we will continue our exploration of love in ancient Rome, delving into the evolution of love celebrations through the ages and the cultural influences that shaped the celebration of love.

Chapter 2: Christian Influence on Love Celebrations
St. Valentine: The Patron Saint of Love

In the tapestry of love celebrations, one figure stands as a symbol of devotion, compassion, and the enduring power of love – St. Valentine. As the patron saint of lovers, his legacy has transcended time and culture, influencing the celebration of love in the Christian tradition. The story of St. Valentine is shrouded in mystery, blending historical accounts, legends, and the collective imagination of generations. In exploring the life and legacy of St. Valentine, we unravel the threads that connect the Christian influence on love celebrations and the timeless ideals of love, compassion, and sacrifice.

The Enigmatic Figure of St. Valentine

St. Valentine, like many early Christian saints, emerges from the shadows of history with a veil of uncertainty surrounding his life and deeds. The lack of definitive historical records has allowed myth and legend to intertwine, creating a narrative that captures the essence of his significance as the patron saint of love.

One prevalent account suggests that St. Valentine was a Roman priest during the third century under the reign of Emperor Claudius II. In a time marked by political instability and military campaigns, Claudius II issued a decree banning marriages for young men, believing that single men made better soldiers. St. Valentine, recognizing the injustice of this decree and guided by compassion, defied the emperor's orders and continued to perform marriages for young couples in secret.

Another legend attributes the association of St. Valentine with love to his acts of kindness and compassion towards prisoners. According to this narrative, St. Valentine, while imprisoned for his Christian beliefs, healed the jailer's blind daughter and sent her a note signed "from your Valentine" before his execution. This act is often considered the origin of the tradition of sending love notes on St. Valentine's Day.

The intertwining narratives surrounding St. Valentine's life capture the essence of love as an act of defiance against injustice and a manifestation of compassion in the face of adversity.

The Martyrdom of St. Valentine: A Sacrifice for Love

The life of St. Valentine is inexorably linked to his martyrdom for his Christian beliefs. While the exact details of his death vary in different accounts, the common thread is his unwavering commitment to love and compassion, even in the face of persecution.

One account suggests that St. Valentine was arrested, imprisoned, and eventually executed for his defiance of Emperor Claudius II's edict regarding marriages. The act of performing marriages in secret, driven by his conviction that love should not be stifled by political decree, led to his imprisonment and eventual martyrdom.

Another account places the emphasis on his compassionate acts toward fellow prisoners. In this narrative, St. Valentine's healing of the jailer's blind daughter and the note he sent before his execution signify the transformative power of love even in the direst circumstances.

Regardless of the specific details, the martyrdom of St. Valentine became a testament to the idea that love, as both a spiritual and earthly force, could endure and triumph over persecution. His sacrifice elevated him to the status of a revered figure in the Christian tradition, inspiring generations to come.

Establishing St. Valentine's Day: A Celebration of Love

The association between St. Valentine and love deepened over the centuries, eventually leading to the establishment of St. Valentine's Day as a day dedicated to love and affection. While the precise origins of the celebration are obscured by the passage of time, the enduring connection between St. Valentine and love became a central theme in medieval and Renaissance literature.

The poet Geoffrey Chaucer, in the 14th century, is often credited with popularizing the association between St. Valentine and romantic love. In his poem "Parliament of Foules," Chaucer links the feast day of St. Valentine with the mating of birds, creating a poetic metaphor for courtship and love. The notion of St. Valentine's Day as a day for expressing love and affection gained traction, spreading throughout medieval Europe.

By the 15th century, St. Valentine's Day had become firmly established as a day for the exchange of love notes and tokens. The practice of sending handwritten messages expressing affection became a cultural phenomenon, with individuals using the occasion to declare their love and devotion to one another. The symbolic act of sending a valentine – a message of love inspired by St. Valentine – became a cherished tradition.

St. Valentine's Day Traditions: Tokens of Love

The celebration of St. Valentine's Day evolved over time, with various traditions and customs becoming integral to the expression of love on this special day. The exchange of valentine cards, often adorned with symbols of love such as hearts and Cupid, became a widespread practice. The handwritten notes, once the primary mode of expression, transformed into intricately designed cards that conveyed sentiments of affection.

The tradition of sending flowers, particularly red roses, on St. Valentine's Day also gained prominence. The red rose, with its association with love and passion, became a symbol of romantic expression. The act of gifting flowers on St. Valentine's Day reflects the enduring connection between nature's beauty and the expression of love.

Gift-giving on St. Valentine's Day expanded to include chocolates, candies, and other tokens of affection. The commercialization of the holiday, particularly in the modern era, has contributed to the proliferation of various gift options, allowing individuals to express their love in diverse and creative ways.

St. Valentine's Day around the World: A Global Celebration of Love

The celebration of St. Valentine's Day extended beyond its European origins, becoming a global phenomenon that transcends cultural boundaries. While the traditions and customs associated with the day may vary, the core theme of expressing love and affection remains a universal aspect of the celebration.

In Japan, for example, St. Valentine's Day is marked by the tradition of women presenting gifts, often chocolates, to men. A month later, on White Day, men reciprocate with gifts for the women who gave them presents on St. Valentine's Day. This unique variation on the celebration highlights the cultural nuances that shape the expression of love around the world.

In South Korea, St. Valentine's Day is just one part of a series of celebrations known as the "love days." These include days dedicated to expressing love for friends, couples, and singles, creating a comprehensive calendar of love-themed events throughout the year.

St. Valentine's Day Controversies: Debates and Criticisms

Despite its widespread popularity, St. Valentine's Day has not been without its controversies and criticisms. Some argue that the commercialization of the holiday has led to an emphasis on material gifts, detracting from the genuine and heartfelt expressions of love. Others contend that the pressure to conform to societal expectations on St. Valentine's Day can contribute to feelings of loneliness or inadequacy.

In recent years, debates have emerged regarding the inclusivity of St. Valentine's Day. Critics argue that the celebration tends to prioritize romantic love, potentially excluding those who are not in romantic relationships. In response, movements promoting the celebration of self-love, friendship, and familial love have gained traction, encouraging a more inclusive perspective on the holiday.

St. Valentine's Day in the Digital Age: Virtual Expressions of Love

The advent of the digital age has transformed the way individuals express their love on St. Valentine's Day. Social media platforms, messaging apps, and virtual cards have become popular mediums for sending expressions of affection. The ease of digital communication has allowed people to connect across distances, making it possible to share love and greetings with friends, family, and partners regardless of geographical location.

The rise of online shopping has also influenced the way individuals choose and send gifts on St. Valentine's Day. E-commerce platforms offer a plethora of options, allowing people to select personalized and meaningful gifts for their loved ones with just a few clicks.

Conclusion: St. Valentine's Legacy of Love

St. Valentine's Day, with its roots in the Christian tradition and the enduring legacy of an enigmatic saint, continues to be a day dedicated to love and affection. The celebration has evolved over the centuries, adapting to cultural changes and expanding its reach across the globe. While debates and criticisms persist, the fundamental theme of expressing love on St. Valentine's Day remains a powerful and cherished tradition that resonates with individuals of diverse backgrounds and beliefs.

As we delve further into the Christian influence on love celebrations, we will explore additional aspects of the interplay between religious traditions and the celebration of love. From the fusion of ancient Roman traditions with Christian ideals to the literary contributions that shaped the cultural understanding of love, our journey through the chapters will unravel the intricate tapestry of love celebrations across the ages.

Christianizing Roman Festivals

In the grand tapestry of love celebrations, the influence of Christianity intertwines with the remnants of ancient Roman traditions, creating a rich and complex mosaic that continues to shape the way we commemorate love today. As Christianity spread across the Roman Empire, it encountered established festivals and traditions dedicated to love and fertility. The process of Christianizing these pagan celebrations involved a delicate dance of adaptation, transformation, and reinterpretation, ultimately giving rise to unique expressions of love within the context of Christian beliefs.

The Challenge of Pagan Festivals: A Christian Perspective

As Christianity gained prominence in the Roman Empire, it encountered a landscape dotted with pagan festivals and traditions deeply ingrained in the social fabric. Many of these festivals, including those dedicated to love and fertility, were associated with deities and rituals that predated the Christian era. The challenge for early Christian leaders was how to integrate these existing celebrations into the emerging Christian narrative while aligning them with Christian values.

One of the primary motivations for Christianizing Roman festivals was to redirect the focus from pagan deities to Christian principles, providing a new spiritual context for celebrations. By appropriating existing festivals and imbuing them with Christian meaning, the early Church sought to facilitate the transition from pagan practices to Christian observances.

Advent of Christianity: The Intersection with Lupercalia

One of the notable instances of Christianizing a Roman festival is the intersection with Lupercalia, an ancient Roman festival dedicated to fertility and purification. Celebrated annually on February 15th, Lupercalia had deep roots in Roman society and was associated with the wolf-goddess Lupa, as well as the she-wolf that, according to legend, nursed Romulus and Remus.

The Christianization of Lupercalia took place in the 5th century when Pope Gelasius I sought to replace the pagan festival with a Christian observance. In an effort to diminish the pagan practices associated with Lupercalia, the Pope established the Feast of the Purification of the Virgin Mary, also known as Candlemas, on February 2nd. This feast commemorated the presentation of Jesus at the temple and the purification of the Virgin Mary after childbirth.

By introducing Candlemas, the Christian Church strategically positioned a significant feast near the time of Lupercalia, redirecting the focus from pagan rituals to the Christian narrative of purification and light. Over time, Candlemas became associated with blessings and processions, effectively transforming the landscape of February celebrations in a Christian direction.

Feast of St. Valentine: A Christian Alternative to Lupercalia

The Christianization of Roman festivals also extended to the establishment of feasts dedicated to Christian saints. The Feast of St. Valentine, observed on February 14th, became a notable Christian alternative to the pagan celebrations of Lupercalia. The association between St. Valentine and love, compassion, and martyrdom provided a Christian context for the commemoration of love during this time.

While the historical details of St. Valentine's life remain shrouded in mystery, the enduring connection between St.

Valentine and love is believed to have contributed to the Christianization of February celebrations. The feast day provided a platform for expressing love and affection within the framework of Christian virtues.

Christian Influence on Love Poetry: Chaucer's Contribution

The Christian influence on love celebrations extended beyond the establishment of feasts and the adaptation of festivals. The realm of literature played a crucial role in shaping the cultural understanding of love within a Christian context. One of the notable contributors to this transformation was Geoffrey Chaucer, the medieval English poet.

Chaucer, writing in the 14th century, is credited with elevating the association between love and Christian ideals. In his work "Parliament of Foules," Chaucer links the feast day of St. Valentine with the mating of birds, creating a poetic metaphor for courtship and love. This literary connection between St. Valentine's Day and romantic love contributed to the gradual cultural shift that embraced the idea of expressing love within a Christian framework.

Chaucer's influence extended beyond poetry to the broader cultural perception of love. His writings, along with those of other poets and authors of the time, helped establish the association between St. Valentine's Day and romantic expressions of love, reinforcing the Christianization of love celebrations.

Courtly Love: A Christianized Approach to Romance

The concept of courtly love, which flourished in medieval European literature, represents another facet of the Christianization of love. Courtly love was characterized by a set of ideals and behaviors that idealized the practice of romantic love within the context of chivalry and Christian morality.

Central to the concept of courtly love was the idea of a chaste and noble admiration from a distance. The lover, often a knight, would express devotion and admiration for a lady of higher social standing, and this admiration was expected to inspire the lover to virtuous deeds. The lady, in turn, would inspire the knight to pursue honor, courage, and service.

While courtly love had its roots in secular literature, its ideals were consistent with Christian ethics. The emphasis on chastity, selfless devotion, and the pursuit of virtuous actions aligned with Christian teachings. As courtly love gained popularity in medieval European culture, it contributed to the Christianized narrative of romantic love, further intertwining the ideals of love and Christian morality.

Christian Marriage Rites: Sacred Unions

The Christianization of love celebrations is perhaps most evident in the transformation of marriage rites. As Christianity became the dominant cultural and religious force in Europe, wedding ceremonies underwent a significant shift, incorporating Christian rituals and symbolism.

The sacrament of marriage, as understood in Christianity, became a sacred union blessed by God. The exchange of vows, which once might have been part of Roman marriage ceremonies, took on a distinctly Christian character. The act of promising to love, honor, and cherish one another became not only a social contract but a covenant under the eyes of God.

The symbolism associated with Christian marriage rituals, such as the exchange of rings, took on spiritual significance. The circular shape of the ring, representing eternity, mirrored the enduring nature of the marital commitment. The pronouncement of the couple as "one flesh" during the ceremony echoed biblical teachings on the unity of marriage.

Christian Love and Compassion: A Divine Model

Central to the Christian influence on love celebrations was the integration of the divine model of love and compassion into the cultural understanding of romantic relationships. Christian teachings emphasize the selfless and sacrificial nature of love, drawing inspiration from the biblical concept of agape love – a deep, unconditional, and benevolent love.

The Christianization of love celebrations encouraged individuals to view their romantic relationships through the lens of divine love. The idea that true love involves self-sacrifice, compassion, and commitment aligned with the Christian virtues of humility and service. This perspective elevated the cultural understanding of romantic love, framing it as a reflection of the divine love modeled by Christ.

Legacy of Christianized Love Celebrations: A Unifying Thread

The Christianization of love celebrations left an indelible mark on the cultural landscape of Europe and beyond. The integration of Christian ideals into the commemoration of love not only transformed existing traditions but also created a unifying thread that connected diverse cultures under a common framework of Christian morality.

St. Valentine's Day, once a Christian alternative to pagan festivals, became a cultural phenomenon that transcended religious boundaries. The association between love and Christian virtues contributed to the enduring popularity of St.

Valentine's Day as a day dedicated to expressing affection and devotion.

The Christianized narrative of love also influenced artistic expressions, literature, and societal norms surrounding romantic relationships. The concept of romantic love, infused with Christian ideals, became a central theme in the cultural imagination, shaping the way individuals approached and understood love in the context of their faith.

Conclusion: Christianization as a Cultural Bridge

The Christianization of love celebrations stands as a testament to the adaptive nature of cultural traditions. By weaving Christian ideals into existing festivals and traditions, early Christian leaders created a cultural bridge that connected the spiritual and the earthly realms. The legacy of this Christianized narrative of love endures, providing a framework for the celebration of love that resonates across diverse cultures and religious beliefs.

As we continue our exploration of Christian influence on love celebrations, the journey will lead us through the literary contributions that shaped the cultural understanding of love, the Renaissance's impact on expressions of affection, and the emergence of Valentine's Day cards as a cultural phenomenon. Each chapter unfolds a new layer of the intricate tapestry of love celebrations through the ages, revealing the interplay between faith, culture, and the enduring human quest for connection and companionship.

Chaucer and the Birth of Valentine's Day Poetry

In the annals of literary history, the 14th-century English poet Geoffrey Chaucer stands as a luminary whose words have left an indelible mark on the cultural understanding of love. Chaucer's contributions to the realm of love poetry, particularly his association of St. Valentine's Day with romantic expressions, played a pivotal role in shaping the trajectory of Valentine's Day as we know it today. As we delve into the nexus of Chaucer's creativity and the emergence of Valentine's Day poetry, we uncover the poetic tapestry that has woven love into the very fabric of this celebrated day.

Chaucer's Literary Landscape: Context and Influences

Geoffrey Chaucer, often hailed as the "Father of English Literature," lived during the 14th century, a time of significant cultural, social, and literary transformation. The medieval period, marked by the remnants of chivalry and the emerging influence of the Renaissance, provided a fertile ground for Chaucer's literary endeavors.

Born into a milieu shaped by courtly love traditions, Chaucer drew inspiration from both classical and contemporary sources. The troubadour tradition, which celebrated the ideals of courtly love through poetry and song, influenced Chaucer's understanding of romantic themes. Additionally, his exposure to Italian literature, particularly the works of Dante and Petrarch, contributed to the nuanced portrayal of love in his writings.

As a courtier and a civil servant, Chaucer navigated the intricacies of the medieval court, gaining insights into the dynamics of love, power, and societal expectations. It is within this rich cultural context that Chaucer embarked on a literary journey that would elevate the association between St. Valentine's Day and romantic poetry.

Parliament of Foules: The Poetic Confluence of Love and Nature

Chaucer's poetic masterpiece, "Parliament of Foules" (Parlement of Foules), serves as a seminal work that marks the birth of Valentine's Day poetry. Composed around 1382, the poem is a testament to Chaucer's artistry in blending classical motifs with contemporary themes, creating a narrative that transcends time and resonates with the enduring nature of love.

The poem is set against the backdrop of the Roman tradition of choosing a mate on St. Valentine's Day. In "Parliament of Foules," Chaucer employs the allegorical device of a dream vision, a popular literary convention of the time. The narrator dreams of an assembly of birds gathering to choose their mates, symbolizing the courtly love conventions prevalent in medieval literature.

The dream unfolds in a natural setting, where the beauty of nature mirrors the complexities of human emotions. Chaucer masterfully intertwines themes of love, desire, and free will, drawing parallels between the avian courtship rituals and the intricate dance of human relationships. The birds' quest for love becomes a metaphor for the timeless pursuit of romantic connection.

The Link to St. Valentine's Day: Chaucer's Artistic Ingenuity

While "Parliament of Foules" doesn't explicitly mention St. Valentine's Day, Chaucer strategically positions the dream vision within the temporal framework of a specific day. The poem is set on the feast day of St. Valentine, adding a layer of significance to the avian courtship rituals. The choice of St.

Valentine's Day as the backdrop aligns with the emerging cultural association of the day with expressions of love.

Chaucer's artistic ingenuity lies in his ability to infuse the narrative with symbolic meaning. The dream vision becomes a vehicle for exploring the complexities of love, drawing a parallel between the avian mating rituals and the human experience of courtship. By situating the poem on St. Valentine's Day, Chaucer elevates the theme of love to a cultural and religious context, contributing to the evolving narrative of the day as a celebration of romantic affection.

The Mating Rituals of Birds: Courtly Love in Nature

"Parliament of Foules" unfolds as the narrator observes a gathering of birds, each species symbolizing different aspects of love and desire. The allegorical portrayal of avian courtship rituals provides a lens through which Chaucer explores the multifaceted nature of human love.

The eagles, representing nobility and high status, engage in a majestic courtship, highlighting the grandeur associated with courtly love. The falcon, embodying beauty and grace, becomes the object of desire for a host of suitors, illustrating the themes of unrequited love and competition. The doves, emblematic of fidelity, demonstrate the enduring nature of love through their committed pairings.

Chaucer's portrayal of avian courtship rituals serves as a reflection of the courtly love conventions prevalent in medieval literature. The birds become allegorical figures, each contributing to the broader narrative of love as a complex and nuanced experience. The blending of nature with the themes of courtly love adds depth to the poetic exploration of romantic relationships.

The Language of Love: Chaucer's Poetic Expression

Chaucer's poetic prowess shines through in the language and imagery employed in "Parliament of Foules." The poem unfolds in rhymed couplets, a stylistic choice that enhances the rhythmic flow of the narrative. Chaucer's use of vivid and evocative language creates a sensory experience for the reader, immersing them in the sights and sounds of the avian courtship spectacle.

The dreamlike quality of the narrative, coupled with Chaucer's keen observations of nature, contributes to the timeless appeal of the poem. The imagery of birds in flight, the vibrant colors of their plumage, and the sounds of their calls become a poetic canvas upon which Chaucer paints a vivid exploration of love's intricacies.

Chaucer's linguistic dexterity extends to the nuanced portrayal of human emotions. The eagerness of the suitors, the hesitations of the pursued, and the dynamics of competition are all captured with a keen understanding of the complexities inherent in matters of the heart. Through his poetic expression, Chaucer invites readers to contemplate the universal themes of love and desire.

Valentine's Day Association: Chaucer's Enduring Impact

While Chaucer's "Parliament of Foules" doesn't explicitly establish St. Valentine's Day as a day for the exchange of romantic expressions, the association between the poem and the cultural celebration of love is undeniable. Chaucer's artistic vision contributed to the evolving narrative of St. Valentine's Day as a time for expressing affection and devotion.

The juxtaposition of the avian courtship rituals with the temporal setting of St. Valentine's Day adds layers of meaning to the poem. Chaucer's creative choice to link the dream vision with the cultural festivities of the day underscores the thematic exploration of love as a central element of human experience.

As the poem gained recognition, the cultural association between St. Valentine's Day and expressions of romantic love continued to solidify. Over time, the day became synonymous with the exchange of love notes, tokens, and sentiments. Chaucer's artistic ingenuity laid the foundation for the poetic tradition of expressing love on St. Valentine's Day, contributing to the emergence of Valentine's Day poetry as a cultural phenomenon.

Chaucer's Legacy: Love, Literature, and Valentine's Day

Geoffrey Chaucer's influence extends beyond the medieval courts of England; it reverberates through the corridors of literary history and the cultural observance of love. His exploration of love in "Parliament of Foules" set the stage for future generations of poets and writers to engage with themes of romance and affection.

Chaucer's impact on the cultural understanding of St. Valentine's Day as a celebration of love endured through the centuries. As the printing press disseminated his works, "Parliament of Foules" reached wider audiences, contributing to the popularization of Valentine's Day traditions. The poem's themes became ingrained in the collective imagination, shaping the way individuals approached expressions of love on this special day.

In the chapters that follow, we will trace the continued evolution of Valentine's Day poetry, exploring how subsequent poets and writers contributed to the rich tapestry of expressions of love. From the Renaissance's poetic revival to the commercialization of Valentine's Day in the modern era, each chapter unravels new threads in the intricate story of love's enduring presence in human culture.

Valentine's Day as a Day of Courtly Love

In the medieval tapestry of love and chivalry, Valentine's Day emerged as a significant canvas on which the ideals of courtly love were painted with poetic finesse. This period, marked by the interplay of Christian morality and the remnants of ancient traditions, saw the cultural elevation of St. Valentine's Day as a day dedicated to the expression of courtly love. As we navigate the corridors of medieval romance, we uncover the nuances of courtly love, its cultural significance, and the lasting impact it had on the celebration of love on this revered day.

Courtly Love: A Cultural Phenomenon

The concept of courtly love, originating in medieval European literature, represented an idealized form of love that elevated the act of loving to a refined and noble pursuit. This cultural phenomenon emerged within the context of chivalric codes, where knights and ladies engaged in a complex dance of emotions characterized by admiration, devotion, and a respectful distance.

Central to courtly love was the idea of a knight expressing his admiration and devotion to a lady of higher social standing. The lady, often unattainable and revered as an ideal, became the object of the knight's chaste and noble affection. The love expressed in courtly love was often unrequited, existing as a poetic and spiritual ideal rather than a consummated physical relationship.

The Idealized Lady: Unattainable Beauty

In the realm of courtly love, the lady held a position of paramount importance. She was not merely an object of desire; she was an idealized figure embodying virtues such as beauty, grace, and moral integrity. The knight, entranced by the lady's qualities, sought to serve her with unwavering loyalty and honor.

The unattainability of the lady added a layer of complexity to courtly love. The knight's affection was often expressed through poetic compositions, gifts, and acts of service. The very act of longing for an unattainable ideal became a source of inspiration for poets and troubadours, shaping the literary landscape of medieval romance.

Chivalric Codes: Love, Honor, and Service

Courtly love was intrinsically connected to the broader chivalric codes that governed the behavior of knights. The knight, inspired by his love for the lady, was expected to demonstrate virtues such as courage, loyalty, and honor in both love and war. The pursuit of excellence in these virtues became a central theme in medieval literature, influencing societal expectations and norms surrounding romantic relationships.

The code of chivalry emphasized the transformative power of love, suggesting that the devotion to a noble and virtuous lady could inspire the knight to reach new heights of moral and martial excellence. The fusion of romantic and martial ideals created a cultural synergy that resonated with the societal aspirations of the medieval elite.

Literary Expressions of Courtly Love: Poetry and Romance

The literary expressions of courtly love reached their zenith in the troubadour poetry of the 11th and 12th centuries. Troubadours, poet-musicians of medieval Occitania, composed lyric poetry that celebrated the ideals of courtly love. Their verses, sung in the courts of nobility, became a cultural phenomenon that transcended regional boundaries.

The troubadour tradition spread throughout medieval Europe, giving rise to similar traditions such as the trouvères in northern France and the minnesingers in Germany. The thematic elements of courtly love, including the idealization of the lady, the concept of "amor de lonh" (distant love), and the use of elaborate metaphorical language, permeated the poetic landscape.

St. Valentine's Day: A Fitting Occasion for Courtly Love

Against the backdrop of this cultural milieu, St. Valentine's Day became a fitting occasion for the expression of courtly love. The association of the day with the commemoration of St. Valentine, often regarded as the patron saint of love, provided a Christian context for the celebration of romantic ideals. The merging of Christian values with the chivalric codes of courtly love created a unique cultural synthesis.

As the celebration of St. Valentine's Day gained popularity, it became intertwined with the poetic expressions of courtly love. The day offered a designated moment for knights and ladies to engage in the ritualized exchange of love tokens, poetic declarations, and symbolic gestures of affection. St. Valentine's Day became a canvas upon which the ideals of courtly love could be painted with the colors of devotion, admiration, and romantic longing.

The Exchange of Valentine's Day Tokens: A Ritual of Affection

The celebration of St. Valentine's Day as a day of courtly love involved the exchange of tokens that conveyed sentiments of affection and admiration. These tokens, often in the form of handwritten notes, love letters, or small gifts, served as tangible expressions of the complex emotions associated with courtly love.

The act of composing and exchanging love notes on St. Valentine's Day mirrored the troubadours' tradition of composing verses dedicated to the idealized lady. Poetic language, rich in metaphor and symbolism, became the vehicle through which courtly love was expressed. The exchange of these tokens created a ritualized practice that added a layer of ceremony to the celebration of love on this special day.

Valentine's Day in Medieval Literature: The Continuation of Tradition

The themes of courtly love found their way into medieval literature, further solidifying the association between St. Valentine's Day and the expression of romantic ideals. Poets and writers continued to explore the complexities of love within the context of courtly love traditions, creating narratives that resonated with the cultural imagination of the time.

One notable example is the 14th-century English poet Geoffrey Chaucer, whose work "Parliament of Foules" explored the themes of courtly love against the backdrop of St. Valentine's Day. Chaucer's poetic vision contributed to the evolving narrative of Valentine's Day as a day dedicated to the expression of romantic affection.

The Legacy of Courtly Love: Shaping the Cultural Landscape

The legacy of courtly love extends beyond the medieval period, leaving an indelible mark on the cultural landscape of love celebrations. The ideals of courtly love, with their emphasis on admiration, devotion, and the pursuit of an unattainable ideal, influenced subsequent generations of poets, writers, and artists.

The chivalric codes that underpinned courtly love continued to shape societal expectations surrounding romantic relationships. While the practice of courtly love evolved over time, its influence persisted in the cultural understanding of love as a noble and transformative force.

Conclusion: Courtly Love and the Cultural Evolution of Valentine's Day

St. Valentine's Day, as a day of courtly love, represents a cultural synthesis that weaves together Christian values, chivalric ideals, and the poetic expressions of medieval romance. The celebration of love on this day became a nuanced tapestry that reflected the complexities of human emotions, from admiration and devotion to the bittersweet beauty of unrequited love.

As we journey through the chapters that follow, we will explore the continued evolution of Valentine's Day celebrations. From the emergence of Valentine's Day cards in the Renaissance to the commercialization of the holiday in the modern era, each chapter unravels new layers in the intricate story of love's enduring presence in human culture.

Chapter 3: Valentine's Day in the Renaissance
The Rise of Valentine's Day Cards

The Renaissance, a period of cultural and intellectual flourishing spanning the 14th to the 17th century, marked a transformative era in the celebration of love and romance. This chapter delves into the emergence of Valentine's Day cards during the Renaissance, a significant development that added a new dimension to the expression of affection. As we explore the cultural and historical context surrounding the rise of Valentine's Day cards, we unravel the intricate threads that wove this tradition into the fabric of the romantic celebrations we know today.

Renaissance Romance: Cultural Context

The Renaissance witnessed a revival of interest in classical art, literature, and humanism, fostering an environment conducive to the exploration of human emotions, including love. The changing cultural landscape was characterized by a shift in artistic and literary expressions, with a renewed focus on individual experiences and emotions.

The courtly love traditions of the medieval period continued to influence the cultural understanding of romance during the Renaissance. However, the Renaissance brought with it a more nuanced and individualistic approach to love, reflecting the broader humanist ideals that emphasized the worth and potential of the individual.

Print Culture and the Spread of Ideas

One of the transformative developments of the Renaissance was the advent of the printing press, invented by Johannes Gutenberg in the mid-15th century. The printing press revolutionized the dissemination of information, making books, pamphlets, and printed materials more widely accessible to the public.

This democratization of information played a crucial role in shaping cultural practices and spreading new ideas. As literacy rates increased and printed materials became more affordable, a burgeoning print culture emerged, fostering the exchange of ideas and influencing societal norms.

Emergence of Valentine's Day as a Cultural Phenomenon

While the association between St. Valentine's Day and love had been established in earlier centuries, it was during the Renaissance that the day gained prominence as a cultural phenomenon celebrating romantic love. The cultural shift toward individualism, the increased accessibility of printed materials, and the flourishing of artistic expression created fertile ground for the growth of Valentine's Day celebrations.

Poets and writers of the Renaissance contributed to the romanticization of St. Valentine's Day through their literary works. The theme of love, often explored through sonnets, poems, and love letters, became a popular subject among the literati of the time. Notable figures such as William Shakespeare, Petrarch, and Edmund Spenser immortalized the themes of love and romance in their writings, influencing the cultural perception of Valentine's Day.

Craftsmanship and Artistry in the Renaissance

The Renaissance was characterized by a renewed emphasis on craftsmanship, artistry, and aesthetics. This focus extended to the creation of handmade tokens and expressions of affection, which became integral to the celebration of love during this period.

The exchange of handwritten love letters, adorned with intricate calligraphy and adorned with symbols of love, became a cherished practice among the literate elite. The craftsmanship and artistry of these personalized missives added a layer of intimacy to the expression of romantic sentiments.

The Precursor to Valentine's Day Cards: Love Letters and Missives

Before the formalized tradition of Valentine's Day cards, the exchange of handwritten love letters served as the primary mode of expressing romantic feelings. These letters were often elaborate, containing carefully crafted prose or poetry expressing the sender's affection and devotion. The personal touch of a handwritten letter, often sealed with wax and decorated with symbols of love, created a tangible and sentimental connection between the sender and the recipient.

As the practice of exchanging love letters gained popularity, it laid the groundwork for the evolution of Valentine's Day cards. The emphasis on personal expression, sentimentality, and the use of artistic elements set the stage for the transition from handwritten letters to more formalized cards.

The Advent of Valentine's Day Cards

The formal exchange of Valentine's Day cards as we know it today finds its roots in the evolving cultural practices of the Renaissance. The tradition of sending cards became more prevalent during the 16th century, and the practice gained momentum in the centuries that followed.

Printed Cards and Commercialization

The printing press played a pivotal role in the widespread availability of Valentine's Day cards. Printed cards allowed for the mass production of designs, making them more affordable and accessible to a broader audience. The commercialization of Valentine's Day cards gained traction as printers and publishers capitalized on the cultural enthusiasm for expressing romantic sentiments.

Printed cards featured intricate designs, often incorporating elements such as cupids, hearts, flowers, and romantic symbols. The imagery and sentiments conveyed on these cards varied widely, catering to different tastes and preferences. The cards provided a canvas for artistic expression, and publishers enlisted skilled artists to create visually appealing and emotionally resonant designs.

Evolution of Card Designs and Themes

As the tradition of sending Valentine's Day cards continued to evolve, the designs and themes of the cards became more diverse. The Victorian era, in particular, witnessed a proliferation of elaborately decorated cards adorned with lace, ribbons, and embossed designs. These ornate cards often featured intricate pop-up elements, adding a three-dimensional quality to the visual appeal.

The language of flowers, known as floriography, became a popular theme in Victorian-era cards. Each flower held symbolic meaning, allowing senders to convey specific emotions through their choice of floral imagery. This nuanced form of communication added an extra layer of sentimentality to the exchange of cards.

Sentiments and Verses: The Poetry of Love Cards

Valentine's Day cards often featured poetic verses expressing sentiments of love, affection, and devotion. These verses ranged from traditional expressions of love to more whimsical and humorous messages. The use of poetry on cards became a means of personalizing the message, providing senders with a way to convey their emotions in a nuanced and eloquent manner.

The practice of including verses on Valentine's Day cards aligns with the historical connection between love and poetry. The tradition of composing love poetry, dating back to the troubadours and courtly love traditions, found a new medium in the written sentiments of Valentine's Day cards.

Social Customs and Card Exchanges

The exchange of Valentine's Day cards became a social custom, particularly among the middle and upper classes. The practice of sending and receiving cards allowed individuals to express their feelings to those they admired or loved. It also provided an opportunity for secret admirers to convey their affections anonymously, adding an element of mystery to the tradition.

Card exchanges were not limited to romantic partners; friends, family members, and acquaintances also participated in the practice. The act of sending cards became a way to strengthen social bonds and express goodwill toward others. The inclusive nature of Valentine's Day card exchanges contributed to the widespread popularity of the tradition.

Innovation in Printing Technology

Advancements in printing technology during the 19th and 20th centuries further transformed the landscape of Valentine's Day cards. The introduction of color printing allowed for vibrant and visually striking designs, expanding the creative possibilities for card manufacturers. The mass production of cards became more efficient, enabling a wider distribution and greater accessibility.

Commercialization and Popularization

The commercialization of Valentine's Day cards continued to escalate, with manufacturers producing cards to suit a range of tastes and preferences. From sentimental and romantic cards to humorous and playful ones, the variety of options catered to diverse expressions of love. The convenience of purchasing pre-made cards made the tradition accessible to a broader audience.

Conclusion: From Handwritten Letters to Global Expressions of Love

The rise of Valentine's Day cards during the Renaissance marked a significant evolution in the cultural expression of love. From the handwritten love letters adorned with craftsmanship and artistry to the mass-produced, commercially available cards of the modern era, the tradition has undergone dynamic changes while retaining its essence.

Valentine's Day cards, with their diverse designs and sentiments, have become a global phenomenon, transcending cultural boundaries. The tradition continues to thrive as an enduring expression of affection, allowing individuals to convey their feelings in a tangible and meaningful way. As we navigate the chapters ahead, we will explore further developments in the celebration of Valentine's Day, including the integration of chocolates, flowers, and other commercial elements into the cultural tapestry of love.

Literary Contributions to Valentine's Day

The Renaissance, a period of cultural rebirth and intellectual awakening, witnessed a profound transformation in the expression of love through literature. Poets, playwrights, and writers of the Renaissance era played a pivotal role in shaping the cultural understanding of Valentine's Day, infusing it with nuanced themes of romance, passion, and the complexities of human relationships. In this exploration of literary contributions to Valentine's Day during the Renaissance, we delve into the works of key figures who left an indelible mark on the celebration of love.

Shakespearean Sonnets: Capturing the Essence of Love

William Shakespeare, often hailed as the bard of the Renaissance, is a towering figure whose works have left an enduring impact on literature and the cultural understanding of love. His collection of 154 sonnets, composed between 1592 and 1598, stands as a masterpiece that delves into the multifaceted nature of love, ranging from idealized beauty to the challenges of passionate relationships.

Sonnet 18: Shall I compare thee to a summer's day?

Shakespeare's Sonnet 18 is perhaps one of the most famous sonnets, capturing the essence of love's timelessness. The speaker begins by contemplating whether to compare the object of his affection to a summer's day but ultimately concludes that the beloved's beauty surpasses the transient glory of the seasons. This sonnet not only celebrates the enduring nature of love but also serves as an ode to the immortalizing power of poetry.

Sonnet 116: Let me not to the marriage of true minds

Sonnet 116, often recited at weddings, explores the steadfast nature of true love. The speaker eloquently declares that love is unchanging and endures despite adversity. The sonnet emphasizes the constancy of love, portraying it as a guiding star that navigates the challenges of time and circumstance. In the context of Valentine's Day, Sonnet 116 reflects the timeless commitment celebrated on this day of love.

Sonnet 130: My mistress' eyes are nothing like the sun

Sonnet 130 takes a more unconventional approach to love poetry by rejecting the conventional tropes of idealized beauty. Instead of comparing his mistress to celestial or natural wonders, Shakespeare's speaker humorously describes her imperfections. The sonnet challenges conventional notions of beauty, presenting a more realistic and down-to-earth portrayal of love.

Shakespeare's sonnets, with their exquisite language and exploration of the human experience of love, contributed to the cultural tapestry of Valentine's Day. As these sonnets circulated in the literary landscape of the Renaissance, they became emblematic of the complex and multifaceted nature of romantic relationships.

Petrarchan Love: Influence on Valentine's Day Imagery

The Petrarchan tradition of love poetry, rooted in the works of the Italian poet Petrarch (1304–1374), also exerted a significant influence on the literary landscape of the Renaissance. Petrarch's collection of sonnets, "Canzoniere" or "Song Book," celebrated his unrequited love for Laura, an idealized and unattainable figure. This theme of unrequited love, combined with the use of elaborate metaphors and allegorical elements, found resonance in the works of Renaissance poets.

Petrarchan imagery often included motifs such as the lover's sighs, the torment of unfulfilled desire, and the symbolism of the lady's beauty as a source of both inspiration and anguish. The Petrarchan conventions of expressing love—coupled with the conventions of courtly love—seeped into the literary expressions of Valentine's Day during the Renaissance.

Edmund Spenser's "The Faerie Queene": Allegorical Romance

Edmund Spenser, another luminary of the Renaissance, contributed to the literary landscape with his epic poem "The Faerie Queene." While not explicitly focused on Valentine's Day, Spenser's work encapsulates the allegorical and chivalric themes prevalent in Renaissance literature.

"The Faerie Queene" explores the virtues of chivalry and the allegorical journey of the Redcrosse Knight, who embodies the ideals of holiness. The intricate narrative weaves together elements of romance, adventure, and moral allegory. Spenser's portrayal of love in "The Faerie Queene" reflects the chivalric ideals of courtly love, adding a layer of complexity to the Renaissance understanding of love and its celebration.

John Donne: Metaphysical Exploration of Love

The metaphysical poets of the 17th century, including John Donne, brought a distinctive style to the exploration of love. Donne's poetry, marked by intellectual rigor and conceit, often delved into the complexities of human relationships, including themes of love, desire, and spiritual connection.

Holy Sonnet 14: Batter my heart, three-person'd God

While not a conventional love poem, Holy Sonnet 14 reflects Donne's exploration of the intense and paradoxical nature of love. The sonnet employs metaphors of warfare and religious devotion to convey the speaker's desire for a transformative experience of divine love. Donne's innovative use of language and metaphor expanded the poetic possibilities for expressing the intricacies of love during the Renaissance.

Donne's broader body of work, including his love poems and religious sonnets, contributed to the intellectual and emotional depth of Renaissance literature. His metaphysical exploration of love influenced subsequent generations of poets, adding a layer of philosophical inquiry to the celebration of love.

Literary Themes and the Cultural Shift in Valentine's Day

The literary contributions to Valentine's Day during the Renaissance marked a cultural shift in the celebration of love. While the medieval period had focused on courtly love traditions and troubadour poetry, the Renaissance brought forth a more individualistic and nuanced approach to love, exploring a range of emotions and experiences.

The themes of unrequited love, the enduring nature of true love, and the complexities of human relationships became central to the literary expressions of Valentine's Day. The Renaissance poets, with their eloquent verses and imaginative metaphors, provided a rich and diverse foundation for the cultural understanding of love that continues to resonate today.

As we traverse through the subsequent chapters, we will further explore the evolution of Valentine's Day celebrations, from the rise of Valentine's Day cards to the commercialization of the holiday in the modern era. Each phase of this cultural journey adds new layers to the intricate story of love's enduring presence in human culture.

Queen Victoria and the Romantic Revival

The Renaissance, a period of cultural and artistic flourishing, marked a renaissance not only in literature but also in the celebration of love. As we delve into the Renaissance's influence on Valentine's Day, a pivotal figure emerges in the 19th century who played a significant role in shaping the romantic sentiments associated with the celebration—Queen Victoria. This section explores Queen Victoria's impact on the Romantic Revival and the enduring influence it had on Valentine's Day traditions.

The Victorian Era: Setting the Stage for Romance

The 19th century, known as the Victorian era, was characterized by a complex interplay of social, cultural, and artistic changes. Queen Victoria, who ascended to the throne in 1837 and reigned until 1901, became a central figure in shaping the values and aesthetics of the time. The Victorian era is often associated with a revival of romantic ideals, emphasizing sentimentality, decorum, and the celebration of love and marriage.

Queen Victoria and Prince Albert: A Romantic Partnership

Queen Victoria's own romantic relationship with her husband, Prince Albert, became a celebrated and influential model for Victorian society. The Queen's intense grief following Albert's death in 1861 elevated their love story to a poignant symbol of enduring devotion. Victoria's mourning and the commemoration of their relationship set a tone for the sentimental expressions of love that would characterize the Victorian approach to romance.

Valentine's Day in Victorian Society

During the Victorian era, Valentine's Day underwent a transformation, evolving into a more elaborate and sentimental celebration. The Victorian preoccupation with romance and courtship manifested in the customs and traditions associated with the holiday. The exchange of Valentine's Day cards, in particular, became a widespread and cherished practice, reflecting the sentimental ideals of the time.

Elaborate Valentine's Day Cards: A Visual Feast

The Victorian era witnessed a significant evolution in the design and production of Valentine's Day cards. These cards became elaborate and visually stunning, featuring intricate lacework, embossing, and colorful illustrations. The use of delicate materials, such as paper lace and satin ribbons, added a tactile and luxurious dimension to the cards.

The imagery on Victorian Valentine's Day cards often incorporated symbols of love, such as cupids, hearts, flowers, and doves. The cards were carefully crafted to convey romantic sentiments, and their ornate designs made them not only tokens of affection but also keepsakes to be treasured.

Sentiments and Poetry: The Language of Love

Victorian Valentine's Day cards were adorned with poetic verses expressing sentiments of love and admiration. The language of love poetry, reminiscent of the courtly love traditions, found a resurgence in the Victorian era. The verses on Valentine's Day cards ranged from tender declarations of affection to playful and humorous messages.

Floral symbolism, known as floriography, also played a prominent role in Victorian Valentine's Day cards. Different flowers carried specific meanings, allowing senders to convey nuanced emotions through their choice of floral imagery. The use of poetry and symbolism added layers of meaning to the exchange of cards, creating a rich tapestry of romantic expression.

Valentine's Day as a Social Event

In Victorian society, Valentine's Day became a social event with its own set of rituals and customs. The exchange of cards extended beyond romantic partners to include friends, family members, and acquaintances. The act of sending and receiving cards was not limited to intimate relationships; it became a way to strengthen social bonds and express goodwill.

Courtship and Romantic Gestures

Valentine's Day in the Victorian era was closely linked to courtship and romantic gestures. Young couples, often guided by the etiquette of the time, engaged in elaborate rituals to express their affection. The exchange of love tokens, handwritten notes, and small gifts became integral to the courtship process, and Valentine's Day provided a designated occasion for these expressions of love.

The Influence of Literature: Romantic Novels and Poetry

The Victorian era was marked by a proliferation of romantic literature, including novels and poetry that explored themes of love, passion, and societal expectations. Authors such as Jane Austen, the Brontë sisters, and Elizabeth Barrett Browning contributed to the romantic literary landscape of the time.

Jane Austen's novels, known for their exploration of love and social dynamics, captured the imagination of Victorian readers. The themes of courtship, marriage, and the complexities of romantic relationships resonated with the societal ideals of the era. Similarly, the works of the Brontë sisters, with their passionate and dramatic portrayals of love, added to the romantic fervor of Victorian literature.

Elizabeth Barrett Browning's famous sonnet sequence "Sonnets from the Portuguese" (1850) expressed profound and sincere emotions of love. The themes of intense devotion and the transformative power of love found resonance with Victorian readers, contributing to the cultural atmosphere that elevated the celebration of love.

The Language of Flowers: Floriography and Sentimental Symbolism

The Victorian fascination with expressing emotions through symbolic gestures extended to the language of flowers, known as floriography. Different flowers carried specific meanings, allowing individuals to convey sentiments without explicitly stating them. This symbolic language found its way into the celebration of Valentine's Day, adding a layer of sentimental meaning to floral gifts and decorations.

Roses, with their association with love and passion, became particularly significant during the Victorian era. The red rose, in particular, symbolized deep love and romance. The exchange of roses on Valentine's Day became a timeless tradition that continues to be a symbol of love today.

The Legacy of Queen Victoria's Romantic Revival

Queen Victoria's influence on the Romantic Revival during the Victorian era left a lasting legacy on the celebration of love, particularly on Valentine's Day. The sentimental and elaborate expressions of affection that characterized the Victorian approach to romance continue to influence contemporary celebrations of love.

The tradition of sending elaborate Valentine's Day cards, adorned with sentimental verses and symbols of love, became ingrained in the cultural practices associated with the holiday. The emphasis on romantic gestures, the exchange of tokens, and the celebration of enduring love can be traced back to the Victorian era.

Conclusion: Queen Victoria's Enduring Influence on Valentine's Day

Queen Victoria's reign marked a pivotal moment in the cultural evolution of Valentine's Day, shaping the celebration into a more elaborate and sentimental affair. The Victorian ideals of love, influenced by the Queen's own romantic experiences, permeated society and contributed to the enduring traditions associated with the holiday.

As we journey through the subsequent chapters, we will explore further developments in the celebration of Valentine's Day. From the commercialization of the holiday to its globalization and contemporary expressions of love, each phase adds new layers to the intricate story of love's enduring presence in human culture.

Valentine's Day Traditions in the 18th and 19th Centuries

As we continue our exploration of Valentine's Day through the lens of history, we enter the 18th and 19th centuries—a period marked by societal changes, cultural shifts, and the evolution of Valentine's Day traditions. In this chapter, we delve into the customs and practices that defined the celebration of love during these centuries, examining how the holiday transformed amidst the backdrop of Enlightenment ideals, the Industrial Revolution, and the burgeoning influence of literature and art.

The Enlightenment and Changing Perspectives on Love

The Enlightenment, an intellectual movement that swept across Europe during the 18th century, brought about a shift in societal attitudes toward love and relationships. Enlightenment thinkers emphasized reason, individualism, and the pursuit of personal happiness. These ideals influenced the perception of love, encouraging a more rational and companionate approach to romantic relationships.

The traditional notion of arranged marriages began to give way to the concept of marrying for love, with individuals seeking compatibility, shared values, and emotional fulfillment in their unions. This changing perspective on love had a ripple effect on how Valentine's Day was celebrated, with an increasing emphasis on personal expressions of affection and sentiment.

The Emergence of Valentine's Day Cards

The 18th century witnessed the rise of Valentine's Day cards as a popular means of expressing affection. Handwritten notes and letters had been exchanged for centuries, but the commercial production of printed cards became more prevalent during this time. The accessibility of printed materials and the growth of the postal system contributed to the widespread popularity of sending Valentine's Day greetings.

Early Valentine's Day cards were often handmade and adorned with intricate designs. The messages ranged from poetic declarations of love to playful and humorous expressions of affection. As the production of cards became more commercialized, a variety of designs and sentiments emerged, catering to different tastes and relationships.

Sentimental Tokens and Love Gifts

In addition to cards, sentimental tokens and small love gifts gained popularity as expressions of affection during the 18th and 19th centuries. Lovers exchanged items such as lockets, rings, and miniature paintings as symbols of their devotion. These tokens often held personal significance, serving as tangible reminders of the emotional bond between the giver and the recipient.

Love gifts were not limited to romantic partners; friends, family members, and acquaintances also exchanged tokens of affection on Valentine's Day. The practice of giving and receiving gifts became an integral part of the holiday, fostering a sense of connection and goodwill among individuals.

Literary Influences: Poetry and Romantic Themes

The Romantic movement, which gained momentum in the late 18th and early 19th centuries, had a profound impact on the cultural expressions of love. Romantic poets, including William Wordsworth, Samuel Taylor Coleridge, and Lord Byron, explored themes of nature, emotion, and the sublime, shaping the literary landscape of their time.

The Romantic poets' emphasis on emotion, individualism, and the transcendental power of love resonated with the evolving celebration of Valentine's Day. Poetic expressions of love, whether inspired by the Romantics or drawn from earlier literary traditions, became a common feature in Valentine's Day cards and notes.

Literary Contributions to Valentine's Day: Percy Bysshe Shelley

Percy Bysshe Shelley, a prominent Romantic poet, made notable contributions to the literary landscape of Valentine's Day. His poem "Love's Philosophy" explores the interconnectedness of nature and love, suggesting that everything in the world is bound by the desire for union. The sentiments expressed in Shelley's poetry aligned with the Romantic ideals of passion and the transcendental nature of love, influencing the thematic content of Valentine's Day cards and messages.

"The fountains mingle with the river, And the rivers with the ocean; The winds of heaven mix forever With a sweet emotion; Nothing in the world is single; All things by a law divine In one another's being mingle:— Why not I with thine?"

Victorian Era: Elaborate Expressions of Love

The Victorian era, spanning much of the 19th century, brought about a heightened emphasis on elaborate expressions of love during Valentine's Day. The societal values of the time, including propriety, sentimentality, and the celebration of domesticity, influenced the customs associated with the holiday.

Victorian Valentine's Day cards became increasingly ornate and intricate. Lace, paper-cut designs, and embossing were common features, adding a touch of elegance to the cards. The language of flowers, known as floriography, became a popular theme, with different flowers carrying specific meanings that allowed senders to convey nuanced emotions.

Love and Courtship: Etiquette and Rituals

In the 18th and 19th centuries, the celebration of Valentine's Day was intertwined with the rituals and etiquette of courtship. Young couples engaged in elaborate practices to express their affection, often guided by societal norms and expectations. The exchange of love tokens, handwritten notes, and small gifts became integral to the courtship process.

Valentine's Day Balls and Social Gatherings

Valentine's Day also became an occasion for social gatherings and events during the 18th and 19th centuries. Balls, parties, and communal celebrations provided individuals with the opportunity to come together, fostering a sense of camaraderie and shared joy. These social gatherings were not limited to romantic partners; they included friends, family, and community members.

Commercialization and Mass Production

The 19th century marked a significant shift in the commercialization of Valentine's Day. The Industrial Revolution played a crucial role in the mass production of cards and love-themed merchandise. Advances in printing technology allowed for the efficient creation of elaborate and visually appealing cards, making them more accessible to a broader audience.

Valentine's Day Poetry: Robert Burns

The influence of literature on Valentine's Day continued with the contributions of Robert Burns, the national poet of Scotland. Burns's poetic works, including his famous song "A Red, Red Rose," conveyed themes of enduring love and passion. The emotional depth and romanticism in Burns's poetry resonated with individuals seeking expressive and heartfelt messages for their loved ones on Valentine's Day.

"O my Luve's like a red, red rose, That's newly sprung in June: O my Luve's like the melodie, That's sweetly play'd in tune."

The Evolution of Valentine's Day Greetings

As the 18th and 19th centuries progressed, the evolution of Valentine's Day greetings reflected the changing cultural landscape. The holiday became an opportunity for individuals to express their emotions through a variety of means, from handwritten notes and love tokens to commercially produced cards and gifts.

Conclusion: Romantic Evolution in the 18th and 19th Centuries

The 18th and 19th centuries witnessed a romantic evolution in the celebration of Valentine's Day. Influenced by Enlightenment ideals, the Romantic movement, and societal changes, the holiday transformed into a more personalized and elaborate expression of affection. The emergence of Valentine's Day cards, sentimental tokens, and the intertwining of literature with the celebration laid the foundation for the diverse and sentimental traditions observed in the modern era.

As we progress through the subsequent chapters, we will explore further developments in the celebration of Valentine's Day. From the commercialization and globalization of the holiday to contemporary expressions of love, each phase adds new layers to the intricate story of love's enduring presence in human culture.

Chapter 4: Commercialization and Modernization
The Industrial Revolution and Mass Production of Valentine's Cards

The 19th century marked a period of profound societal and economic transformations with the advent of the Industrial Revolution. As industries flourished and technology advanced, the way people celebrated Valentine's Day underwent a significant evolution. In this chapter, we explore the impact of the Industrial Revolution on the mass production of Valentine's Day cards, examining how this technological revolution influenced the accessibility and commercialization of expressions of love.

The Industrial Revolution: Catalyst for Change

The Industrial Revolution, which began in the late 18th century and continued well into the 19th century, ushered in a new era characterized by mechanization, urbanization, and unprecedented technological advancements. The shift from agrarian economies to industrialized societies had far-reaching effects on various aspects of daily life, including the way people communicated and celebrated special occasions.

The Rise of Print Culture

One of the key outcomes of the Industrial Revolution was the rise of print culture. The development of printing technologies, such as the steam-powered printing press, enabled the mass production of printed materials at a scale previously unimaginable. Newspapers, magazines, and books became more accessible to the general public, fostering a culture of literacy and information exchange.

This proliferation of printed materials extended to the realm of personal communication, including the exchange of greetings and sentiments on occasions like Valentine's Day. The

Industrial Revolution played a pivotal role in transforming the nature of these personal expressions, leading to the emergence of commercially produced Valentine's Day cards.

Early Commercialization: Handmade to Mass-Produced

Prior to the Industrial Revolution, Valentine's Day cards were often handmade, personalized expressions of affection. The tradition of exchanging handwritten notes, letters, and tokens of love had deep historical roots. However, as the demand for Valentine's Day greetings increased with the growing literacy rates and cultural emphasis on sentimental expressions, the need for a more efficient means of production became apparent.

The shift from handmade to mass-produced Valentine's Day cards was facilitated by innovations in printing technology. The ability to reproduce images and text rapidly and in large quantities revolutionized the way sentiments of love were conveyed. While early examples of commercial Valentine's Day cards retained a degree of craftsmanship, the transition to mass production paved the way for greater accessibility and affordability.

Lithography and Decorative Techniques

Lithography, a printing technique that involved creating images on flat surfaces with a greasy substance, played a crucial role in the production of early mass-produced Valentine's Day cards. This method allowed for the creation of detailed and intricate designs, giving rise to visually appealing cards that could be reproduced in large quantities.

The cards were often adorned with decorative elements, including embossing, foil, and intricate paper-cut designs. These embellishments added a touch of elegance and sophistication to the cards, making them desirable tokens of affection. The use of lithography and decorative techniques contributed to the artistic evolution of Valentine's Day cards, transforming them from simple written notes to visually captivating expressions of love.

Esther Howland: Pioneer of Commercial Valentine's Day Cards

One of the trailblazers in the commercialization of Valentine's Day cards was Esther Howland, an American entrepreneur and artist. In the mid-19th century, Howland, inspired by an English Valentine's Day card she received, saw the commercial potential of producing similar cards for the American market.

Howland, operating her business in Worcester, Massachusetts, is often credited with popularizing the commercial Valentine's Day card industry in the United States. Her cards were known for their elaborate designs, featuring lace, colorful illustrations, and sentimental verses. Howland's innovative approach to marketing and distribution, including the use of sales agents and catalogs, contributed to the widespread popularity of her cards.

The Floral Language: Symbolism and Sentiment

Flowers have long been associated with expressions of love and emotion, and their symbolic meanings were particularly emphasized in Victorian culture. The mass production of Valentine's Day cards during the Industrial Revolution often incorporated intricate floral designs, with each flower carrying specific sentiments.

The language of flowers, known as floriography, allowed individuals to convey nuanced emotions without explicitly stating them. Roses, in particular, became synonymous with love, passion, and romance. The ability to reproduce detailed and symbolic floral imagery on mass-produced cards added a layer of meaning to the visual language of love.

Cultural Impact: Expressing Emotion at Scale

The mass production of Valentine's Day cards had a profound cultural impact by democratizing the expression of love. No longer confined to the elite or those with artistic skills, the general public could now easily access and share sentiments of affection. The ability to express emotions at scale transformed the nature of personal communication and contributed to the commercialization of Valentine's Day as a widely celebrated holiday.

Global Reach: Expanding Markets and Cultural Exchange

The mass production of Valentine's Day cards also facilitated the globalization of the holiday. As cards were produced in large quantities and distributed widely, the cultural exchange of romantic sentiments transcended geographical boundaries. The standardized imagery and messages on these cards created a universal language of love that resonated across diverse cultures.

Valentine's Day, once rooted in specific cultural and historical traditions, became a global phenomenon. The exchange of cards allowed people from different parts of the world to participate in a shared celebration of love, contributing to the holiday's enduring popularity on an international scale.

Evolution of Designs: From Victorian Elegance to Modern Trends

The evolution of Valentine's Day card designs reflects not only changes in printing technology but also shifts in artistic trends and cultural preferences. While Victorian-era cards were characterized by intricate lacework, embossing, and sentimental verses, the 20th century witnessed a diversification of styles.

Art Deco influences in the early 20th century brought about geometric patterns and bold designs, departing from the ornate aesthetics of the Victorian era. As the century progressed, mid-century modern and pop art movements introduced new visual languages that found expression in Valentine's Day cards. The embrace of humor, simplicity, and contemporary themes added a dynamic element to the designs.

Conclusion: The Legacy of Mass-Produced Valentine's Day Cards

The Industrial Revolution's impact on the mass production of Valentine's Day cards transformed the holiday from a personalized, handmade tradition to a commercially accessible and widely celebrated event. The technological innovations of the time not only made expressions of love more convenient but also contributed to the cultural evolution of Valentine's Day as a global celebration.

As we navigate through the subsequent chapters, we will explore further developments in the commercialization and modernization of Valentine's Day. From the emergence of the floral industry to the integration of candies, chocolates, and other commercial elements into the celebration, each phase adds new layers to the intricate story of love's enduring presence in human culture.

Emergence of the Floral Industry on Valentine's Day

The commercialization of Valentine's Day did not stop with the mass production of cards; it extended to encompass the floral industry, adding a fragrant and visually stunning dimension to the celebration of love. In this chapter, we explore the fascinating history of how flowers, particularly roses, became synonymous with Valentine's Day and how the floral industry bloomed into a multi-billion-dollar enterprise, shaping the way people express and symbolize their affections.

Flowers as Symbols of Love: A Historical Perspective

The association between flowers and expressions of love dates back centuries, with different cultures attributing specific meanings to various blooms. In ancient Rome, flowers were used to honor the goddess Venus, the embodiment of love and beauty. Similarly, in medieval Europe, the language of flowers, known as floriography, allowed individuals to convey emotions through carefully chosen blooms.

During the Renaissance, the exchange of flowers gained popularity as a romantic gesture. The emphasis on courtly love and chivalry elevated flowers to symbols of admiration and devotion. By the 18th and 19th centuries, books on the language of flowers became popular, guiding individuals in selecting the appropriate blooms to express their sentiments.

Roses: The Quintessential Symbol of Love

Among all flowers, the rose emerged as the preeminent symbol of love and passion. This iconic status can be traced back to ancient mythology, where the rose was associated with Aphrodite, the Greek goddess of love. In Roman times, roses were linked to Venus, her Roman counterpart.

The red rose, in particular, became a powerful symbol of deep love and desire. Its rich color and velvety petals captured the essence of romance, making it the perfect representation of affection and devotion. As Valentine's Day evolved, the red rose would come to dominate the floral landscape of the holiday.

Early Floral Expressions on Valentine's Day

While the exchange of flowers on Valentine's Day predates the commercialization of the holiday, it was not until the 19th century that the floral industry began to capitalize on the romantic sentiments associated with the celebration. Early floral expressions were often modest, with individuals choosing and presenting flowers to convey their feelings.

The sentiment behind floral gifts was deeply intertwined with the language of flowers. Each type of flower carried a specific meaning, allowing senders to communicate nuanced emotions without uttering a word. For example, the red rose signified passionate love, while other flowers like violets, lilies, and daisies conveyed sentiments ranging from faithfulness to innocence.

Floral Sentiments in Victorian Culture

The Victorian era, with its emphasis on sentimentality and elaborate expressions of emotion, elevated the exchange of flowers to an art form. Victorian society placed great importance on proper etiquette and symbolic gestures, and flowers provided a language through which individuals could communicate their feelings.

Floral bouquets became elaborate arrangements, carefully crafted to convey specific messages. The art of floriography reached its zenith during this period, with guidebooks and dictionaries helping people decode the meanings of different flowers. The act of presenting a carefully arranged bouquet became a powerful way to express love, admiration, or friendship.

Influence of Literature: Poetry and Flowers

Literary works of the time, particularly poetry, played a significant role in perpetuating the association between flowers and romantic love. Poets like Lord Byron, Robert Burns, and John Keats often wove floral imagery into their verses, further cementing the link between blooms and passionate emotions.

For example, in Lord Byron's poem "She Walks in Beauty," the beauty of the subject is compared to the night and stars, culminating in the lines:

"And on that cheek, and o'er that brow, So soft, so calm, yet eloquent, The smiles that win, the tints that glow, But tell of days in goodness spent,— A mind at peace with all below, A heart whose love is innocent!"

Such poetic expressions, coupled with the Victorian fascination with romantic literature, contributed to the popularity of flowers as tokens of affection.

Esther Howland and the Floral Valentine

Esther Howland, a key figure in the commercialization of Valentine's Day cards, also played a role in popularizing the combination of flowers with these cards. Howland's elaborate Valentine's Day cards often featured three-dimensional floral designs, enhancing the visual appeal of her creations. Her innovative approach set the stage for the integration of flowers into the broader Valentine's Day gifting tradition.

The Rise of the Floral Industry: 19th Century

The emergence of the floral industry on Valentine's Day can be traced to the 19th century, where societal changes, technological advancements, and the commercialization of the holiday converged. With the rise of urbanization and the expansion of transportation networks, flowers could be grown, harvested, and transported more efficiently, making them accessible to a wider audience.

Florists capitalized on the growing popularity of Valentine's Day by offering pre-arranged bouquets and floral designs specifically tailored for the occasion. The convenience of purchasing professionally arranged flowers appealed to individuals seeking to make a memorable and expressive gesture of love.

The Language of Roses: Red Roses Reign Supreme

While various flowers were exchanged on Valentine's Day, it was the red rose that emerged as the undisputed symbol of romantic love. The deep red hue of the rose, coupled with its association with passion and desire, made it the quintessential choice for expressing deep affection.

The tradition of presenting red roses on Valentine's Day gained momentum in the 19th century and has endured as a timeless symbol of love. The act of giving a single red rose or a bouquet of red roses became synonymous with romantic intentions, conveying a depth of emotion that transcended words.

Floral Arrangements and Bouquets: A Visual Language of Love

The art of crafting floral arrangements and bouquets took center stage as florists sought to create visually stunning and meaningful compositions. The careful selection of flowers based on their meanings allowed senders to convey specific sentiments. For instance, a bouquet featuring red roses, symbolizing love, could be complemented by white lilies for purity or baby's breath for innocence.

The diversity of floral arrangements catered to the preferences and personalities of both the sender and the recipient. Some arrangements emphasized elegance and sophistication, while others embraced a more natural and wild aesthetic. The language of flowers became a visual poetry, with each arrangement telling a unique love story.

Floral Innovations: Preserving and Enhancing Beauty

Advancements in floral preservation techniques, such as drying and pressing, allowed individuals to extend the lifespan of their Valentine's Day bouquets. Pressed flowers could be incorporated into cards or framed, serving as lasting mementos of love. Additionally, the introduction of hothouse cultivation enabled the availability of certain flowers year-round, further expanding the choices for Valentine's Day floral gifts.

Commercialization and Modern Trends

As the floral industry on Valentine's Day continued to grow, it became increasingly integrated into the broader commercial landscape. Floral shops, both local and chain retailers, capitalized on the holiday's association with romantic gestures. Pre-ordering arrangements, delivery services, and themed floral promotions became common practices, catering to the convenience-seeking consumer.

The introduction of themed arrangements and mixed bouquets allowed for creative expression beyond the traditional red rose bouquet. Floral designers embraced a variety of blooms, colors, and textures, offering options that appealed to a diverse range of tastes. From classic and elegant to contemporary and avant-garde, the floral industry adapted to changing aesthetics and preferences.

Impact of Mass Media: Reinforcing Floral Traditions

The 20th century saw the rise of mass media, including radio, television, and later the internet, which played a pivotal role in reinforcing and perpetuating Valentine's Day floral traditions. Advertisements, films, and popular culture consistently depicted the exchange of flowers as a romantic and meaningful gesture, further embedding these practices into societal norms.

Television shows and movies often featured scenes of characters exchanging bouquets of flowers on Valentine's Day, contributing to the cultural expectation that flowers were an essential element of the celebration. Advertisements by florists emphasized the emotional impact of floral gifts, positioning them as indispensable expressions of love and affection.

International Influence: Globalization of Floral Practices

The globalization of Valentine's Day, coupled with the international flower trade, contributed to the standardization of floral practices across cultures. Red roses, in particular, became a universal symbol of love, transcending linguistic and cultural barriers. The floral industry adapted to this globalized approach, with similar floral arrangements and themes being marketed and embraced worldwide.

Challenges and Criticisms: Environmental and Ethical Concerns

While the floral industry on Valentine's Day thrived commercially, it also faced scrutiny and criticisms. Environmental concerns related to the carbon footprint of importing flowers, particularly out-of-season varieties, raised questions about sustainability. Additionally, ethical issues surrounding labor practices and fair wages within the global flower trade became points of contention.

These challenges prompted discussions about the ecological and social impact of the floral industry, leading to increased awareness and efforts to promote environmentally friendly and ethically sourced flowers. Sustainable practices, such as supporting local flower growers and opting for seasonal blooms, gained traction as individuals sought to align their expressions of love with broader ethical considerations.

Conclusion: The Blooming Legacy of Valentine's Day Flowers

The emergence of the floral industry on Valentine's Day is a testament to the enduring power of symbolism and the dynamic interplay between culture, commerce, and tradition. From the ancient associations of flowers with love to the Victorian fascination with floriography, the integration of flowers into the celebration of Valentine's Day has evolved into a global phenomenon.

As we navigate through the subsequent chapters, we will further explore the commercialization and modernization of Valentine's Day. From the integration of candies and chocolates to the impact of technology on contemporary expressions of love, each phase adds new layers to the intricate story of love's enduring presence in human culture.

Candy, Chocolates, and Valentine's Day

The sweet symphony of love found its perfect accompaniment with the integration of candies and chocolates into the celebration of Valentine's Day. In this chapter, we explore the delectable history of how these sugary delights became inseparable from expressions of affection, creating a multi-billion-dollar industry that has sweetened the language of love for generations.

The Sweet Beginnings: Early Traditions of Sweet Gifts

The exchange of sweet treats as expressions of affection has roots that stretch far back in history. In medieval Europe, courtly love traditions often involved the exchange of confections and sweetened beverages. The symbolic gesture of offering sweets to a beloved was considered a token of one's admiration and romantic interest.

As sugar became more widely available in Europe during the Renaissance, the popularity of sweet gifts continued to grow. Elaborate sugar sculptures and marzipan creations adorned feasts and celebrations, symbolizing not only indulgence but also the sweetness of love.

Sugar, Chocolate, and the European Sweet Tooth

The introduction of sugar and chocolate to Europe from the Americas in the 16th and 17th centuries marked a transformative moment in the history of sweet indulgences. Sugar, initially a luxury reserved for the elite, became more accessible as production methods improved and trade routes expanded.

Chocolate, originally consumed as a beverage, underwent innovations in processing, making it more palatable and versatile. By the 18th century, chocolate began to be molded into solid forms, paving the way for the creation of the first chocolate bars.

Chocolate and Love: A Delicious Duo

The association between chocolate and love can be traced back to the Aztecs, who believed that chocolate had aphrodisiac properties. The European elite, enamored with the exoticism of chocolate, embraced it as a luxury beverage associated with indulgence and romance.

By the 19th century, the perception of chocolate as a romantic gift had solidified. Boxes of chocolates, often beautifully decorated, became popular tokens of affection exchanged between lovers. The Victorians, known for their elaborate expressions of sentiment, embraced the tradition of presenting chocolate as a sweet declaration of love.

Richard Cadbury and the Heart-Shaped Box

The iconic heart-shaped box of chocolates, now synonymous with Valentine's Day, owes its popularity to Richard Cadbury. In the mid-19th century, Cadbury, a British chocolatier and son of the founder of Cadbury chocolate company, introduced the first heart-shaped box filled with assorted chocolates.

Cadbury's innovative packaging transformed the presentation of chocolates into a visual feast. The heart-shaped box, adorned with romantic imagery and sentiments, became a symbol of love and elegance. This marketing strategy not only contributed to the commercial success of Cadbury but also established a lasting tradition in the celebration of Valentine's Day.

Milton S. Hershey: Chocolate for the Masses

While the tradition of exchanging chocolates on Valentine's Day gained traction among the elite, it was the vision of Milton S. Hershey that democratized chocolate consumption. Hershey, an American entrepreneur, revolutionized the chocolate industry by introducing mass production techniques.

Hershey's commitment to affordability and accessibility made chocolate a treat for the masses. The introduction of the Hershey's Kisses in 1907, individually wrapped bite-sized chocolates, added a playful element to chocolate gifting and contributed to the popularization of Hershey's chocolates as an accessible and beloved Valentine's Day treat.

The Rise of Commercial Brands: Valentine's Day Marketing

The mid-20th century witnessed the rise of commercial chocolate brands leveraging the sentimentality of Valentine's Day for marketing purposes. Brands like Godiva, Ferrero Rocher, and Lindt positioned their premium chocolates as the epitome of indulgence and luxury, appealing to consumers seeking to express their love through gourmet treats.

Valentine's Day marketing campaigns, often featuring romantic imagery, couples, and heart motifs, created a powerful association between chocolates and expressions of love. The practice of gifting chocolates on Valentine's Day became deeply ingrained in popular culture, transcending socio-economic boundaries.

Chocolates as Love Tokens: Meaning Behind the Treats

Beyond their delicious taste, chocolates became imbued with symbolic meaning in the context of romantic gestures. The act of gifting chocolates on Valentine's Day conveys thoughtfulness, sweetness, and a desire to indulge and pamper a loved one. The variety of chocolates within a box often reflects a range of emotions, from the creamy and comforting to the rich and intense.

Innovations in Chocolate: Artistry Meets Indulgence

The world of chocolate has evolved beyond traditional bars and boxes. Artisanal chocolatiers and gourmet chocolate makers have pushed the boundaries of creativity, infusing chocolates with unique flavors, textures, and designs. Handcrafted chocolates, often presented in visually stunning packaging, elevate the act of chocolate gifting to an art form.

From infused truffles to sculpted chocolate figures, these artisanal creations cater to individuals seeking a more personalized and exquisite chocolate experience. The intersection of artistry and indulgence has given rise to a culture of appreciating chocolate as both a sensory delight and a form of edible art.

International Influences: Global Diversity in Chocolates

The globalization of the chocolate industry has brought forth a diverse array of chocolates, each reflecting the cultural preferences and tastes of different regions. In Japan, for example, the tradition of giri-choco (obligation chocolate) involves women giving chocolates to men on Valentine's Day as a social obligation. In contrast, many Western cultures embrace the exchange of chocolates as a mutual expression of love between partners.

The incorporation of local flavors, traditional ingredients, and regional preferences has led to the creation of unique chocolate experiences worldwide. This diversity enriches the global celebration of Valentine's Day, offering a wide spectrum of chocolate options that cater to various tastes and cultural contexts.

Candy: A Playful Addition to Valentine's Day

While chocolates exude a sense of sophistication and indulgence, candies inject an element of playfulness into the celebration of love. The tradition of exchanging candy on Valentine's Day has deep historical roots, with early confections often being handmade and shared among friends and loved ones.

The commercialization of candies for Valentine's Day gained momentum in the 20th century. Brands like conversation hearts, small heart-shaped candies with printed messages, became iconic symbols of the holiday. The playful and whimsical nature of candies added a lighthearted touch to the traditional exchange of romantic sentiments.

The Evolving Landscape of Sweet Treats: Dietary Trends and Preferences

In contemporary times, the landscape of sweet treats for Valentine's Day has evolved to accommodate changing dietary trends and preferences. The demand for alternatives such as vegan, gluten-free, and sugar-free options has led to the development of a diverse range of confections that cater to individuals with specific dietary restrictions.

Artisanal candy makers and chocolatiers now offer innovative options, incorporating ingredients like coconut sugar, plant-based milk, and alternative sweeteners. This inclusivity ensures that individuals with dietary preferences or restrictions can still partake in the joy of indulging in sweet treats on Valentine's Day.

Challenges and Criticisms: Health and Ethical Concerns

While the sweet indulgence of candies and chocolates is a beloved tradition, it is not without its share of challenges and criticisms. Health concerns, particularly related to excessive sugar consumption and its impact on overall well-being, have prompted discussions about the need for moderation in indulging in sweet treats.

Additionally, ethical concerns within the chocolate industry, such as child labor and sustainability issues, have raised awareness about the need for responsible and ethical sourcing practices. Consumers are increasingly seeking products that align with their values, prompting the industry to address these concerns and adopt more socially and environmentally responsible practices.

Conclusion: Savoring the Sweet Symphony of Love

The integration of candies and chocolates into the celebration of Valentine's Day has transformed these sugary delights into more than just confections; they have become integral components of the language of love. From the historic exchange of sweet gifts in medieval Europe to the modern tradition of presenting heart-shaped boxes filled with chocolates, these treats have evolved alongside societal changes and continue to be cherished symbols of affection.

As we traverse through the subsequent chapters, we will delve into further dimensions of the commercialization and modernization of Valentine's Day. From the industrial revolution's impact on the production of Valentine's Day cards to the globalization of love celebrations, each phase adds new layers to the intricate story of love's enduring presence in human culture.

Valentine's Day in the 20th Century

The 20th century witnessed a significant transformation in the celebration of Valentine's Day, marking an era of widespread commercialization and modernization. As societal norms evolved, the holiday underwent changes that reflected the cultural shifts, technological advancements, and consumer-driven influences of the time. In this chapter, we explore the key developments that shaped Valentine's Day during the 20th century, from the emergence of popular culture influences to the impact of mass media on the expression of love.

The Consumer Culture Boom: Post-World War II Prosperity

The post-World War II period ushered in an era of unprecedented economic growth and prosperity in many Western countries. This period of affluence, often referred to as the "economic miracle," saw a surge in consumer spending and the emergence of a robust consumer culture.

Valentine's Day, already well-established as a day for expressions of love, became increasingly intertwined with consumerism. The availability of disposable income allowed individuals to indulge in elaborate gestures of affection, including the purchase of commercially produced Valentine's Day cards, chocolates, and other gifts. The holiday, once celebrated with handmade tokens of love, became an opportunity for lavish displays of affection through store-bought items.

Greeting Cards: The Rise of Mass-Produced Sentiments

The mid-20th century witnessed a boom in the mass production of greeting cards, including those dedicated to Valentine's Day. Companies like Hallmark and American Greetings became synonymous with the business of sentiments, offering a wide array of pre-designed cards catering to various relationships and emotions.

The convenience of ready-made cards resonated with the time-pressed urban population. The availability of diverse designs and messages allowed individuals to choose cards that best conveyed their feelings. The practice of exchanging Valentine's Day cards became less about personal expression and more about selecting from the commercially available sentiments, contributing to the standardization of romantic expressions.

Media Influence: Romantic Imagery in Film and Television

The 20th century saw the rise of mass media, particularly film and television, as powerful influencers of cultural norms and societal behaviors. Romantic narratives depicted on the silver screen and television dramas shaped perceptions of love and romance, influencing the way individuals approached Valentine's Day.

Hollywood played a significant role in popularizing grand romantic gestures and the notion of an idealized, cinematic love. Scenes of characters exchanging flowers, chocolates, and heartfelt cards on Valentine's Day became iconic representations of romantic love. The influence of media on Valentine's Day was not just about the products associated with the holiday but also about the idealized expectations and expressions of love that were portrayed.

Commercialization of Romantic Symbols: Red Roses and Cupid

The 20th century solidified certain symbols as synonymous with Valentine's Day, contributing to their commercialization. Red roses, inspired by historical and literary associations with love, became the quintessential flower for expressing romantic affection. The demand for red roses on Valentine's Day soared, leading to the cultivation and distribution of millions of these blooms around the holiday.

Cupid, the mischievous Roman god of love, also became an enduring symbol of Valentine's Day. Depicted as a cherubic figure with a bow and arrow, Cupid's image adorned cards, decorations, and advertisements. The commercialization of these symbols not only fueled the floral and gifting industries but also created a visual language that transcended cultural boundaries.

Fashioning Romantic Traditions: Candlelit Dinners and Jewelry

The 20th century witnessed the establishment of certain romantic traditions associated with Valentine's Day. Candlelit dinners, often portrayed in romantic films and embraced as a symbol of intimate dining, became a popular way for couples to celebrate the occasion. Restaurants capitalized on this tradition by offering special Valentine's Day menus and promotions, further contributing to the commercialization of the holiday.

Jewelry also became a prominent expression of love and commitment during the 20th century. The exchange of engagement rings and other jewelry items on Valentine's Day gained momentum, with jewelers marketing their products as timeless symbols of enduring love. The association between jewelry and romantic gestures contributed to the commodification of expressions of love.

The Technological Revolution: Changing Modes of Communication

The latter half of the 20th century saw the advent of the technological revolution, particularly the rise of personal computing and the internet. These technological advancements transformed the way people communicated and, subsequently, the way they expressed love on Valentine's Day.

The introduction of email and electronic messaging allowed for quicker and more immediate expressions of affection. Virtual cards, often animated and interactive, became a popular alternative to traditional paper cards. The ease of sending digital greetings contributed to the modernization of Valentine's Day expressions, as individuals embraced the convenience of online communication.

Shifting Gender Roles: Women as Active Participants

The 20th century also witnessed significant shifts in gender roles, with women increasingly taking on more active roles in relationships. This change had a notable impact on Valentine's Day, as women began to actively participate in the planning and execution of romantic gestures.

While the traditional expectation was for men to be the primary initiators of romantic expressions, the 20th century saw a more egalitarian approach to celebrating love. Women took on the role of gift-givers, planners of special experiences, and active participants in expressing affection. This shift reflected broader changes in societal expectations around gender roles and relationships.

Counterculture Movements: Challenging Conventional Celebrations

The latter part of the 20th century also saw the rise of counterculture movements that challenged conventional norms, including those associated with Valentine's Day. Some individuals and groups rejected the commercialization of the holiday, viewing it as a manufactured celebration that placed undue pressure on individuals to conform to societal expectations.

Anti-Valentine's Day sentiments emerged, with some people using the occasion to critique consumerism and challenge traditional notions of romance. These counterculture movements added a layer of complexity to the celebration of Valentine's Day, highlighting the diverse ways in which individuals approached the holiday.

Globalization of Love: Valentine's Day Beyond Borders

As the 20th century drew to a close, the globalization of culture and commerce had a profound impact on the celebration of Valentine's Day. The holiday, once predominantly observed in Western countries, became a global phenomenon. The exchange of cards, flowers, and gifts on February 14th transcended cultural and geographical boundaries.

The globalization of Valentine's Day was facilitated by mass media, international travel, and the interconnectedness of the global economy. Different cultures embraced and adapted the holiday, incorporating local traditions and customs into the celebration. The standardization of romantic symbols and expressions contributed to a shared global language of love.

Conclusion: A Century of Love in Transition

The 20th century marked a transformative period in the celebration of Valentine's Day, shaping it into the commercialized and modernized holiday that is familiar to us today. The influence of mass media, the rise of consumer culture, and shifts in societal norms all played crucial roles in defining how love was expressed on February 14th.

As we progress through the subsequent chapters, we will explore further dimensions of the commercialization and modernization of Valentine's Day. From the industrial revolution's impact on the production of cards and the globalization of love celebrations to the contemporary expressions influenced by technology, each phase adds new layers to the intricate story of love's enduring presence in human culture.

Chapter 5: Globalization of Love Celebrations
Valentine's Day Around the World

Valentine's Day, once a celebration rooted in Western traditions, has evolved into a global phenomenon that transcends cultural and geographical boundaries. In this chapter, we embark on a journey around the world to explore how different cultures have embraced, adapted, and personalized the celebration of love on February 14th. From unique customs and traditions to regional variations in expressions of affection, the globalization of Valentine's Day has given rise to a rich tapestry of love celebrations.

Asia: Blending Tradition with Modern Romance

In many Asian countries, Valentine's Day has been embraced as a modern celebration of love, often influenced by Western cultural trends. In Japan, the celebration unfolds in two parts: on February 14th, women traditionally present gifts, often chocolates, to men. A month later, on March 14th, known as White Day, men reciprocate with gifts, completing the cycle of romantic gestures.

South Korea adds an additional layer with Black Day on April 14th, where those who did not receive gifts on Valentine's Day or White Day gather to eat black bean noodles, commiserating with others who may not have found love during the earlier celebrations.

In contrast, some countries in Asia have chosen to put their own spin on Valentine's Day. In China, the celebration has been embraced with enthusiasm, with couples exchanging gifts and enjoying romantic dinners. The Chinese Qixi Festival, often referred to as Chinese Valentine's Day, falls on the seventh day of the seventh lunar month, emphasizing the star-crossed love between a cowherd and a weaver girl.

Europe: Diverse Traditions and Romantic Escapades

Europe, with its rich tapestry of cultures and histories, boasts diverse traditions and expressions of love on Valentine's Day. In the United Kingdom, the day is marked by the exchange of cards, flowers, and romantic gestures. France, often hailed as the epitome of romance, embraces the celebration with passion, and couples exchange gifts and indulge in romantic dinners.

In Denmark and Norway, Valentine's Day is a relatively recent import, and the celebration is characterized by the exchange of white flowers called snowdrops. In Wales, the celebration is intertwined with St. Dwynwen's Day, where love spoons are exchanged, each spoon carrying a symbolic meaning.

Eastern European countries like Romania and Bulgaria have their own unique traditions. In Romania, young couples celebrate the day of Dragobete, the protector of love, with various customs. Bulgaria, on the other hand, observes a day known as Trifon Zarezan, where the focus is on the celebration of wine, fertility, and love.

Latin America: Passionate Celebrations and Cultural Blends

Valentine's Day in Latin America is marked by vibrant and passionate celebrations. In countries like Mexico, couples exchange flowers, chocolates, and other tokens of affection. The day is also an occasion for elaborate romantic gestures, such as marriage proposals and grand declarations of love.

Brazilian celebrations often extend beyond couples to include family and friends. Dia dos Namorados, celebrated on June 12th, precedes Valentine's Day and is a day when people express love and affection for their partners. The celebration culminates in a festive atmosphere with parties, music, and dancing.

Argentina, with its rich cultural history, has embraced Valentine's Day with a unique twist. In addition to the traditional celebrations, there is a week-long celebration known as Sweetness Week, where couples exchange candies and sweets to express their love.

Middle East: Modern Expressions in Traditional Settings

In the Middle East, where cultural traditions play a significant role, Valentine's Day has found its place alongside traditional celebrations of love. In countries like the United Arab Emirates and Saudi Arabia, the day is marked by the exchange of gifts, flowers, and romantic dinners. However, public displays of affection may be more reserved in adherence to cultural norms.

In Iran, where public celebrations of Valentine's Day were historically discouraged, there has been a shift in recent years. Young couples increasingly embrace the day as an opportunity to express their love, often in private settings.

In Israel, Tu B'Av, celebrated in late summer, has been likened to Valentine's Day. The day is associated with love and matchmaking, and it has become a popular time for weddings and romantic events.

Africa: Cultural Diversity in Love Celebrations

Across the diverse nations of Africa, Valentine's Day is celebrated in various ways, blending cultural traditions with modern expressions of love. In South Africa, the day is marked by the exchange of flowers, cards, and gifts, similar to Western traditions.

Nigeria, with its rich cultural tapestry, has embraced Valentine's Day with enthusiasm. The day is celebrated with the exchange of gifts, romantic dinners, and the expression of love through various means. In some regions, traditional customs are integrated into the celebration, adding a unique flavor to the day.

In Ethiopia, where the celebration of love is deeply rooted in the culture, a local holiday known as Timkat, celebrating the Epiphany, often coincides with Valentine's Day. While the celebrations are distinct, the shared focus on love and community ties them together.

North America: Diverse Expressions in the United States and Canada

In the United States and Canada, Valentine's Day is widely celebrated with a focus on romantic expressions. The exchange of cards, flowers, and gifts is a common practice, and romantic dinners or getaways are popular among couples.

However, within North America, there are variations in how different communities celebrate. In the United States, for example, Valentine's Day is not only a celebration of romantic love but also an occasion for friends and family to exchange tokens of affection. The tradition of exchanging valentines in schools further emphasizes inclusivity.

Canada, with its multicultural landscape, sees diverse expressions of love on Valentine's Day. Different cultural communities may incorporate their own traditions and customs into the celebration, creating a mosaic of love that reflects the country's rich diversity.

Oceania: Island Celebrations and Cultural Influences

In the islands of Oceania, Valentine's Day is embraced with a blend of Western influences and local traditions. In

Australia and New Zealand, the day is marked by the exchange of cards, gifts, and romantic gestures. The celebration often extends to include friends and family.

In the Pacific Islands, where cultural traditions are deeply ingrained, Valentine's Day may be celebrated in unique ways. The day becomes an opportunity for communities to come together, share love and goodwill, and express appreciation for one another.

Global Icons of Love and Romance

As Valentine's Day became a global celebration, certain locations gained iconic status as romantic destinations. Cities like Paris, known as the City of Love, and Venice, with its romantic canals, became popular choices for couples seeking a romantic getaway. The allure of these destinations, often perpetuated by popular culture, has contributed to their status as global icons of love and romance.

The concept of "love locks" on bridges, where couples attach padlocks as a symbol of their everlasting love, became a global phenomenon. While some locations embraced this tradition, others grappled with the practical challenges and structural concerns posed by the accumulating weight of the locks.

Controversies and Criticisms Worldwide

While Valentine's Day is widely celebrated, it is not without controversies and criticisms. In some cultures and communities, the commercialization of the holiday has been met with resistance. Critics argue that the emphasis on expensive gifts and grand gestures can create unrealistic expectations and contribute to feelings of inadequacy for those unable to afford lavish displays of affection.

Certain religious and conservative groups in various parts of the world view Valentine's Day as a Western import that conflicts with traditional values. In some cases, public celebrations of the holiday have faced opposition, leading to restrictions on certain activities or public displays of affection.

Conclusion: A Global Tapestry of Love

The globalization of Valentine's Day has transformed the celebration of love into a global tapestry, woven with diverse threads of culture, tradition, and modern expressions of affection. From the bustling streets of Tokyo to the romantic canals of Venice, the universality of love has found expression in myriad ways.

As we journey through the subsequent chapters, we will explore the contemporary expressions of love influenced by technology, changing dynamics of romantic relationships, and the scientific perspectives on love. Each phase adds new dimensions to the intricate story of how love has evolved and continues to thrive across time and borders.

Cultural Adaptations and Traditions

Valentine's Day, as it traverses cultural and geographical boundaries, undergoes fascinating adaptations and assimilations into existing traditions. This chapter delves into the diverse ways in which different cultures have incorporated and shaped the celebration of love, demonstrating the resilience of local customs in the face of global influences.

Japan: The Art of Giri-Choco and Honmei-Choco

In Japan, Valentine's Day has taken on a distinctive and nuanced form of expression. The celebration is characterized by the exchange of chocolates, with a unique twist. Women, both in personal and professional settings, participate in the tradition of "giri-choco," where they give obligatory chocolates to male colleagues and friends. This practice is considered a social duty rather than a romantic gesture.

On the other hand, "honmei-choco" refers to chocolates given to a person with whom the giver has romantic feelings. These chocolates are often handmade, representing a deeper level of affection. The celebration doesn't stop there; a month later, on White Day, men reciprocate by giving gifts to the women who gave them chocolates on Valentine's Day.

This nuanced approach to Valentine's Day in Japan reflects the cultural emphasis on social obligations and the subtleties of expressing romantic feelings.

South Korea: Love and Tradition on White Day

Valentine's Day in South Korea unfolds uniquely with a multi-step celebration that spans February and March. Similar to Japan, women in South Korea initiate the festivities by presenting chocolates to men on Valentine's Day. However, the focus shifts to White Day on March 14th, when men reciprocate by giving gifts, often white chocolates or other white-themed items, to women.

Additionally, there's a twist for those who may not have received gifts on Valentine's Day or White Day. On Black Day, celebrated on April 14th, individuals who didn't participate in the earlier exchanges gather to eat jajangmyeon, a dish of black bean noodles. This unconventional approach to Valentine's Day acknowledges and includes those who may not have had romantic experiences during the preceding celebrations.

China: Embracing a Western Tradition with a Chinese Flavor

Valentine's Day, known as "Qixi" in China, has a rich cultural backdrop. The celebration is based on the legend of Niulang and Zhinü, two lovers separated by the Milky Way who are allowed to reunite only once a year on the seventh day of the seventh lunar month.

In contemporary China, Valentine's Day is embraced with fervor, and young couples exchange gifts, flowers, and chocolates. While the celebration incorporates elements of Western traditions, the Chinese Qixi Festival retains its distinct cultural significance, blending ancient folklore with modern expressions of love.

India: Traditional Roots and Modern Expressions

In India, a country with a deep cultural and religious tapestry, Valentine's Day has made its way into the social calendar, particularly among the younger generation. The celebration often involves the exchange of flowers, cards, and gifts, with couples expressing their affection in various ways.

However, the celebration of love in India is not confined to Valentine's Day alone. The country has its own rich tradition of love stories, prominently featured in mythology and folklore.

The stories of Radha and Krishna, Laila and Majnu, and Heer and Ranjha have inspired generations, adding layers of cultural richness to the expression of love in India.

Brazil: Love, Samba, and Carnivals

In Brazil, the celebration of love extends beyond the confines of Valentine's Day. While February 14th is recognized as a day for expressing affection, Brazilian couples have another opportunity for romantic celebrations on Dia dos Namorados, celebrated on June 12th.

Dia dos Namorados precedes Valentine's Day and has become a day for couples to exchange gifts, enjoy romantic dinners, and partake in festive celebrations. The celebration often culminates in lively samba dances and vibrant carnivals, infusing the expression of love with the exuberance of Brazilian culture.

France: The Epitome of Romance

France, often hailed as the epitome of romance, embraces Valentine's Day with an unmistakable flair. The French celebration is marked by the exchange of flowers, particularly red roses, and the indulgence in romantic dinners. Couples often take the opportunity to express their love with poetic sentiments and grand gestures.

However, France has its own unique celebration of love known as la Fête des Amoureux, celebrated on May 1st. On this day, lovers exchange lily of the valley flowers, a symbol of luck and devotion. This additional celebration showcases the French commitment to expressing love in various ways throughout the year.

Ethiopia: Blending Cultural Traditions

In Ethiopia, where the celebration of love is deeply rooted in culture, the local holiday of Timkat often coincides with Valentine's Day. Timkat, the Ethiopian Orthodox celebration of the Epiphany, involves vibrant processions, religious ceremonies, and communal gatherings. While distinct from Valentine's Day, the shared focus on love and community highlights the ability of cultures to blend and coexist.

Middle East: Navigating Traditions with Modern Celebrations

The celebration of Valentine's Day in the Middle East involves a delicate balance between cultural traditions and modern expressions of love. In countries like the United Arab Emirates and Saudi Arabia, where public displays of affection may be more reserved, couples find ways to express their love within the bounds of cultural norms.

In Iran, where public celebrations of Valentine's Day were historically discouraged, there has been a shift in recent years. Young couples increasingly embrace the day as an opportunity to express their love, often in private settings, reflecting a subtle adaptation of global celebrations to local cultural contexts.

United States: A Melting Pot of Love Traditions

In the United States, a melting pot of cultures, Valentine's Day is celebrated with diverse traditions and expressions of love. The exchange of cards, flowers, and gifts is a common practice, and romantic dinners or getaways are popular among couples.

One unique tradition that has gained popularity is the exchange of "Valentines." This tradition has its roots in the 19th century when people began exchanging handmade cards, often adorned with lace, ribbons, and romantic verses. Today, the tradition continues with the exchange of cards, not just among couples but also among friends and family.

Global Icons of Love: Cities and Symbols

As Valentine's Day became a global celebration, certain locations gained iconic status as romantic destinations. Cities like Paris, known as the City of Love, and Venice, with its romantic canals, became popular choices for couples seeking a romantic getaway. The allure of these destinations, often perpetuated by popular culture, has contributed to their status as global icons of love and romance.

The concept of "love locks" on bridges, where couples attach padlocks as a symbol of their everlasting love, became a global phenomenon. While some locations embraced this tradition, others grappled with the practical challenges and structural concerns posed by the accumulating weight of the locks.

Controversies and Criticisms Worldwide

While Valentine's Day is widely celebrated, it is not without controversies and criticisms. In some cultures and communities, the commercialization of the holiday has been met with resistance. Critics argue that the emphasis on expensive gifts and grand gestures can create unrealistic expectations and contribute to feelings of inadequacy for those unable to afford lavish displays of affection.

Certain religious and conservative groups in various parts of the world view Valentine's Day as a Western import that conflicts with traditional values. In some cases, public celebrations of the holiday have faced opposition, leading to restrictions on certain activities or public displays of affection.

Conclusion: Love's Resilience in Cultural Diversity

The cultural adaptations and traditions surrounding Valentine's Day showcase the resilience of love in the face of diverse cultural contexts. From Japan's nuanced approach to

South Korea's multi-step celebration, and from France's poetic expressions to Brazil's lively carnivals, love finds expression in myriad ways.

As we navigate through the subsequent chapters, we will explore the contemporary expressions of love influenced by technology, changing dynamics of romantic relationships, and the scientific perspectives on love. Each phase adds new dimensions to the intricate story of how love has evolved and continues to thrive across time and borders.

Global Icons of Love and Romance

As Valentine's Day transcends cultural and geographical boundaries, certain locations and symbols have emerged as global icons of love and romance. These destinations and traditions, often perpetuated by popular culture, evoke a sense of timeless and universal love. In this section, we embark on a journey to explore the iconic places and symbols that have become synonymous with expressions of love around the world.

Paris: The City of Love

No discussion of global icons of love would be complete without mentioning Paris, often hailed as the City of Love. The French capital, with its charming streets, iconic landmarks, and romantic ambiance, has captivated lovers for centuries. From the Eiffel Tower, illuminated against the night sky, to the quaint Montmartre district, Paris provides an enchanting backdrop for romantic escapades.

Couples from around the world flock to Paris to celebrate milestones in their relationships, propose marriage, or simply bask in the city's amorous atmosphere. The Seine River, meandering through the heart of Paris, offers boat cruises that allow couples to enjoy breathtaking views of the city's landmarks while savoring a romantic dinner.

The tradition of "love locks" on bridges, particularly the Pont des Arts, became a global phenomenon. Couples would attach padlocks to the bridge's railing, symbolizing their everlasting love, and then throw the key into the Seine River. While the practice faced concerns about the weight and structural integrity of the bridges, it became an enduring symbol of love in the City of Light.

Venice: Romance on the Canals

Venice, with its intricate network of canals, historic architecture, and timeless beauty, is another global icon of love and romance. The city's narrow waterways, gondola rides, and charming piazzas create an enchanting atmosphere that has inspired poets, artists, and lovers for centuries.

Couples meander through the labyrinthine streets, crossing arched bridges and exploring hidden corners. The Grand Canal, the city's main waterway, is adorned with magnificent buildings that add to the romantic allure. Sunset gondola rides, serenaded by the gondoliers, provide an intimate and picturesque experience for couples.

Venice's appeal as a romantic destination is amplified during events like the Venetian Carnival, where masked couples traverse the city's streets, adding an element of mystery and allure. The timeless beauty of Venice has made it a destination for weddings, proposals, and unforgettable moments of love.

Santorini: Whitewashed Romance

The Greek island of Santorini, with its whitewashed buildings perched on cliffs overlooking the Aegean Sea, has become an iconic destination for romantic getaways. The stunning sunsets over the caldera, with hues of pink, orange, and purple painting the sky, create a mesmerizing backdrop for couples.

The villages of Oia and Fira, with their narrow pathways and charming architecture, offer a romantic setting for strolls and candlelit dinners. Luxury resorts carved into the cliffs provide panoramic views of the sea, creating an intimate and exclusive atmosphere for couples seeking a romantic escape.

Santorini's popularity as a destination for weddings and honeymoons has grown, and the island's distinctive aesthetic has been immortalized in countless photographs, paintings, and cinematic scenes. The combination of natural beauty and architectural elegance has solidified Santorini as a global icon of romantic destinations.

Rome: Eternal Love in the Eternal City

Rome, often referred to as the Eternal City, is a treasure trove of history, culture, and romance. With its ancient ruins, Baroque fountains, and charming piazzas, Rome provides a timeless backdrop for expressions of love. The iconic Colosseum, Roman Forum, and Pantheon transport visitors to the heart of ancient history.

The Spanish Steps, adorned with blooming flowers in the spring, have been a meeting place for lovers for centuries. Throw a coin into the Trevi Fountain, according to tradition, and ensure your return to Rome. The city's culinary delights, from gelato to pasta, add a flavorful dimension to romantic experiences.

Rome's role in cinematic love stories, such as in "Roman Holiday" and "La Dolce Vita," has contributed to its image as a city where love unfolds in a grand and unforgettable manner. The juxtaposition of ancient architecture and modern vitality makes Rome a symbol of eternal love.

Kyoto: Tranquil Elegance in Japan

Kyoto, the cultural heart of Japan, offers a serene and elegant setting for expressions of love. The city's traditional wooden machiya houses, historic temples, and beautiful gardens create an atmosphere of tranquility and beauty. Kyoto's cherry blossoms in spring and vibrant autumn foliage add seasonal charm to the city's allure.

The Fushimi Inari Shrine, with its iconic torii gates, provides a picturesque backdrop for couples seeking a blend of cultural richness and natural beauty. The Arashiyama Bamboo

Grove and the historic Gion district offer enchanting settings for romantic strolls.

The practice of "hanami," or cherry blossom viewing, is a cherished tradition in Kyoto, where couples gather to appreciate the fleeting beauty of the blossoms. Kyoto's cultural heritage, reflected in its tea ceremonies, traditional arts, and historical architecture, has made it a destination where love is celebrated with elegance and grace.

New York City: Urban Romance and Time Square

In the bustling metropolis of New York City, urban romance takes center stage. The city's iconic skyline, illuminated by the lights of Times Square, creates a vibrant and dynamic backdrop for expressions of love. From the historic Central Park to the modern High Line, New York City offers diverse settings for romantic escapades.

Times Square, known as "The Crossroads of the World," is a symbol of energy and excitement. Couples often find themselves captivated by the dazzling billboards, Broadway shows, and the electric atmosphere. The city's observation decks, such as the Empire State Building and One World Observatory, provide panoramic views that add a touch of grandeur to romantic moments.

Central Park, with its meandering pathways, picturesque bridges, and iconic landmarks like Bethesda Terrace, offers a natural oasis within the urban landscape. The city's diverse culinary scene, from fine dining to food trucks, allows couples to savor a variety of experiences.

Love Locks and Bridges

The tradition of attaching padlocks to bridges as a symbol of everlasting love has become a global phenomenon. While the practice faced challenges due to concerns about the weight and structural integrity of bridges, it became a symbolic gesture embraced by couples worldwide.

Paris's Pont des Arts, with its thousands of love locks, became an iconic location for this tradition. Couples would attach locks to the bridge's railing, often inscribed with their names or initials, and then throw the key into the Seine River. The symbolism of the love lock transcended Paris and spread to other cities with famous bridges, including the Ponte Vecchio in Florence, Brooklyn Bridge in New York City, and the Milvio Bridge in Rome.

The act of attaching a love lock to a bridge, a tangible expression of commitment and unity, reflects the universal desire for enduring love. While some locations embraced the tradition, others implemented measures to preserve the structural integrity of their bridges.

Heart-Shaped Symbols and Love Arches

Around the world, heart-shaped symbols and love arches have become prominent features in celebrations of love. These iconic structures often serve as backdrops for proposals, weddings, and romantic gestures.

The Love Lock Bridge in Cologne, Germany, features a heart-shaped grid where couples can attach love locks. The Hohenzollern Bridge, adorned with thousands of colorful padlocks, has become a symbol of enduring love.

Love arches, such as the Tunnel of Love in Klevan, Ukraine, create enchanting passageways surrounded by greenery. These natural or man-made arches evoke a sense of romance and have become popular spots for couples to declare their love.

Conclusion: Eternal Symbols of Love

The global icons of love and romance, from the City of Love to enchanting bridges adorned with love locks, serve as eternal symbols of love's enduring power. Whether in the historic streets of Rome or the modern skyline of New York City, these iconic locations transcend cultural boundaries, inviting couples to create timeless moments of love.

As we progress through the subsequent chapters, we will explore the contemporary expressions of love influenced by technology, changing dynamics of romantic relationships, and the scientific perspectives on love. Each phase adds new dimensions to the intricate story of how love has evolved and continues to thrive across time and borders.

Controversies and Criticisms Worldwide

As Valentine's Day has become a global celebration, it has not been immune to controversies and criticisms. The universal themes of love and romance that the day represents are often intertwined with cultural, social, and economic complexities, giving rise to debates and discussions around the world. In this section, we delve into the controversies and criticisms surrounding Valentine's Day on a global scale.

Commercialization and the Pressure to Spend

One of the primary criticisms leveled against Valentine's Day is the pervasive commercialization that accompanies the celebration. Critics argue that the day has transformed into a consumer-driven event, with a strong emphasis on the exchange of gifts, cards, flowers, and chocolates. The pressure to conform to societal expectations and purchase tokens of affection can create a sense of obligation and financial strain for individuals.

In many countries, the weeks leading up to Valentine's Day witness an influx of advertisements promoting romantic gifts, special offers, and exclusive experiences. The commodification of love has been particularly criticized for fostering unrealistic expectations, with elaborate gestures and expensive gifts often portrayed as the standard expression of affection.

Cultural Clashes and Opposition to Western Influences

Valentine's Day, originating from Western traditions, has faced resistance and criticism in some parts of the world where it clashes with existing cultural values and norms. In certain conservative societies, the public celebration of love is viewed as a foreign import that contradicts traditional values.

For example, in countries with predominantly Islamic cultures, public displays of affection may be considered inappropriate or even offensive. As a result, Valentine's Day celebrations in these regions may be more subdued, celebrated privately, or face restrictions imposed by authorities.

In India, where traditional values and customs play a significant role in societal norms, some groups have opposed the adoption of Valentine's Day. These cultural clashes highlight the tension between globalized expressions of love and the preservation of local cultural identities.

Loneliness and Exclusion

While Valentine's Day is marketed as a celebration of love, it can inadvertently accentuate feelings of loneliness and exclusion, particularly for individuals who are not in romantic relationships. The pervasive imagery of happy couples exchanging gifts and enjoying romantic moments may contribute to a sense of inadequacy or societal pressure for those who are single.

In response to this criticism, there has been a growing movement to redefine Valentine's Day as a broader celebration of all forms of love, including platonic, familial, and self-love. Initiatives promoting self-care, community engagement, and inclusive celebrations have sought to alleviate the sense of exclusion that some individuals may experience on Valentine's Day.

Environmental Concerns: The Impact of Excessive Consumption

The mass production of Valentine's Day cards, flowers, and other gifts has raised environmental concerns. The production, packaging, and transportation of these items contribute to carbon emissions, deforestation, and waste generation.

Critics argue that the environmental impact of Valentine's Day has been overlooked in the pursuit of consumer-driven celebrations. The disposal of single-use items, particularly plastics and wrapping materials, adds to the burden on landfills and oceans. In response to these concerns, there has been a growing interest in sustainable and eco-friendly alternatives for celebrating love, such as choosing locally sourced or recycled gifts.

Challenges to Gender Stereotypes

Valentine's Day has often been criticized for perpetuating traditional gender stereotypes, particularly in the portrayal of men as the primary gift-givers and women as the receivers. The expectation that men should make grand gestures and lavish gifts on their partners reinforces gender norms that may not align with evolving views on equality and relationships.

In response to these criticisms, there has been a push for more inclusive and gender-neutral representations of love. Efforts to challenge stereotypes include campaigns promoting shared responsibilities in relationships and encouraging diverse expressions of affection that go beyond traditional gender roles.

Religious Opposition and Moral Concerns

In certain religious communities, Valentine's Day has faced opposition on moral and religious grounds. Some conservative groups view the celebration as promoting premarital relationships and casual dating, which may conflict with their religious teachings.

In countries where conservative interpretations of Islam prevail, for example, religious authorities may discourage or prohibit the celebration of Valentine's Day. Similar sentiments are echoed in some Christian communities that associate the day with secularism and decadence.

Public Health Concerns: Risks of Excessive Revelry

Valentine's Day celebrations, often involving gatherings, parties, and public displays of affection, have occasionally raised public health concerns. In some regions, authorities have expressed worries about the potential spread of infections, particularly during flu seasons or times of heightened health risks.

The consumption of excessive alcohol, a common element in many celebrations, can also contribute to public safety concerns. Authorities may implement measures such as increased policing, traffic regulations, and public awareness campaigns to mitigate these risks during Valentine's Day celebrations.

Legal and Ethical Issues: Exploitation in the Commercial Sector

The commercialization of Valentine's Day has, at times, led to legal and ethical concerns related to exploitative practices. Issues such as price gouging on flowers, inflated costs of romantic dinners, and misleading marketing tactics have prompted regulatory scrutiny in some jurisdictions.

Consumer protection agencies and watchdog organizations have occasionally intervened to address unethical practices, ensuring that businesses adhere to fair pricing and transparent marketing. These legal and ethical challenges underscore the delicate balance between commerce and the genuine celebration of love.

Conclusion: Navigating the Complexities of Love Celebrations

The controversies and criticisms surrounding Valentine's Day on a global scale highlight the complex interplay between cultural traditions, commercial interests, and societal expectations. While the day is intended to celebrate love in its various forms, it often finds itself at the crossroads of competing values, leading to debates about authenticity, inclusivity, and the impact of consumerism.

As we delve into the subsequent chapters exploring the evolution of love celebrations, we will uncover how modernity, technology, and shifting cultural dynamics continue to shape the ways in which love is expressed and celebrated across time and borders.

Chapter 6: Contemporary Expressions of Love
Technological Influences on Modern Romance

In the rapidly evolving landscape of modern romance, technology has emerged as a powerful force shaping the way individuals connect, communicate, and express love. From the early days of online dating to the integration of social media into relationships, technology has revolutionized the dynamics of contemporary love. In this section, we explore the multifaceted impact of technology on modern romance, examining how digital innovations have both facilitated and transformed the ways people experience and express love.

Online Dating: The Digital Path to Love

The advent of the internet has transformed the dating landscape, offering individuals a digital platform to connect with potential partners. Online dating platforms, ranging from early websites like Match.com to the contemporary swipe-right culture of apps like Tinder, have reshaped the way people initiate romantic relationships.

Online dating provides a vast pool of potential matches, allowing individuals to connect with others beyond their immediate social circles. The algorithms employed by dating apps use personal preferences, interests, and geographical location to suggest potential matches, streamlining the process of finding compatible partners.

While online dating has democratized access to romance, it has also raised concerns about authenticity and the potential for deceptive profiles. Users navigate a virtual realm where carefully curated profiles may not always reflect the realities of individuals' lives, introducing an element of uncertainty and, at times, disappointment.

Long-Distance Love: Navigating Relationships Across Borders

Technology has played a pivotal role in bridging the gap for couples in long-distance relationships. Video calls, instant messaging, and social media platforms have become lifelines for those separated by geographical distances, enabling real-time communication and the sharing of daily experiences.

Platforms like Skype, FaceTime, and Zoom have allowed couples to engage in virtual dates, celebrate special occasions together, and maintain a sense of connection despite physical separation. Social media platforms, with their instantaneous sharing of photos and updates, create a virtual space for couples to stay involved in each other's lives.

However, long-distance relationships facilitated by technology also come with their challenges. The absence of physical proximity and the reliance on digital communication can create a sense of emotional distance. Trust, effective communication, and shared goals become even more critical in sustaining a healthy long-distance relationship.

Social Media and Relationship Visibility

The integration of social media into daily life has profoundly impacted how individuals navigate and showcase their romantic relationships. Platforms like Facebook, Instagram, and Twitter provide a public stage for individuals to share their love stories, milestones, and everyday moments with a wide audience.

Couples often document their relationship journey on social media, sharing photos, status updates, and declarations of love. This visibility can serve as a form of digital affirmation, reinforcing the bond between partners and inviting the support and well-wishes of friends and family.

However, the public nature of social media also introduces complexities. The pressure to present an idealized version of a relationship may contribute to feelings of inadequacy or insecurity. Additionally, the sharing of personal details online raises questions about privacy and the potential impact of public scrutiny on intimate relationships.

Virtual Celebrations and Shared Online Spaces

Technology has become an integral part of celebrating special occasions in modern relationships. Whether it's a virtual birthday party, an online anniversary celebration, or a shared gaming experience, couples increasingly utilize digital platforms to create meaningful and interactive moments together.

Video conferencing platforms, in particular, have become a popular medium for virtual celebrations. Couples separated by distance can join in the festivities, participate in virtual games, and share the joy of special occasions in real-time. Online platforms also offer opportunities for collaborative activities, such as watching movies together or engaging in virtual travel experiences.

Shared online spaces, such as collaborative documents, digital photo albums, or joint playlists, provide couples with a virtual canvas to create and curate shared memories. These digital artifacts become a testament to the unique ways in which couples navigate and express their love in the digital age.

Dating Apps and the Changing Landscape of Intimacy

The rise of dating apps has not only transformed how people meet but has also influenced the dynamics of intimacy within relationships. Apps that cater to specific preferences or interests allow individuals to find partners who align with their values and lifestyles.

However, the gamification and instant gratification aspects of some dating apps have raised concerns about the commodification of intimacy. The emphasis on quick matches, casual encounters, and the swipe culture may contribute to a more transactional approach to relationships, challenging traditional notions of courtship and romance.

Conversely, dating apps have also provided a platform for individuals with specific relationship preferences or non-traditional lifestyles to connect with like-minded partners. The increased visibility and acceptance of diverse relationship models, including polyamory and open relationships, reflect the evolving landscape of intimacy facilitated by technology.

Digital Tokens of Affection: Emojis and GIFs

The language of love in the digital age often involves the creative use of emojis, GIFs, and stickers. These digital expressions, embedded in text messages and online communication, add a layer of playfulness and emotion to digital conversations.

Couples use heart emojis, kissing faces, and other symbols to convey affection and sentiment in a concise and visually appealing manner. The use of GIFs allows individuals to express specific emotions or reactions, creating a unique and dynamic form of digital communication.

However, the reliance on digital symbols also raises questions about the depth of emotional expression in online communication. While emojis and GIFs offer a convenient way to convey feelings, some argue that they may lack the nuance and authenticity of face-to-face communication.

Augmented Reality and Virtual Reality Experiences

As technology advances, augmented reality (AR) and virtual reality (VR) have started to play a role in creating immersive romantic experiences. VR, in particular, allows couples to engage in virtual dates, explore digital landscapes together, or attend virtual events as if they were physically present.

AR applications enable users to overlay digital elements onto the real world, opening up possibilities for unique and personalized romantic gestures. For example, AR apps can create virtual trails of messages or digital surprises that appear when viewed through a smartphone.

While these technologies offer innovative ways for couples to connect, they also raise questions about the potential for virtual experiences to replace or overshadow real-world interactions. Striking a balance between the digital and physical realms becomes essential in maintaining the authenticity of romantic relationships.

Challenges and Concerns: Navigating the Digital Landscape

While technology has undeniably enriched the landscape of modern romance, it also introduces challenges and concerns that couples must navigate. Issues such as digital privacy, the impact of social media on relationships, and the potential for online interactions to replace face-to-face connections require thoughtful consideration.

The phenomenon of "phubbing" (phone snubbing), where individuals prioritize their smartphones over face-to-face interactions, has become a concern in relationships. Establishing boundaries for technology use, particularly during quality time together, is crucial to fostering a healthy balance between the digital and physical aspects of a relationship.

Additionally, the permanence and accessibility of digital communication raise questions about the potential consequences of impulsive or thoughtless interactions. Misunderstandings that arise from text messages or social media posts may have lasting impacts on relationships, emphasizing the importance of clear and effective communication.

Conclusion: Navigating the Digital Landscape of Love

Technology has ushered in a new era of possibilities and complexities in the realm of modern romance. From the way people meet and connect to the daily expressions of love, technology has become an integral part of the romantic journey. As we delve into the subsequent chapters exploring the scientific perspectives on love and the enduring symbolism of love traditions, we will continue to uncover the intricate ways in which love evolves and thrives across time and borders, shaped by the interplay of tradition and innovation.

Changing Dynamics of Romantic Relationships

In the evolving landscape of contemporary romance, the dynamics of romantic relationships are undergoing significant transformations influenced by societal shifts, cultural changes, and individual preferences. This section explores the multifaceted aspects of how romantic relationships have evolved, examining topics such as changing societal norms, the redefinition of traditional gender roles, and the pursuit of diverse relationship models.

Shifting Societal Norms: Redefining Love and Partnership

Modern romantic relationships are navigating the currents of shifting societal norms, challenging traditional expectations and embracing a more inclusive and diverse understanding of love. As societies become more accepting of different forms of relationships, individuals are redefining the structures and dynamics that govern their partnerships.

The dismantling of societal taboos surrounding non-traditional relationships, such as same-sex partnerships, polyamory, and open relationships, reflects a broader embrace of diverse expressions of love. Couples are increasingly free to define the parameters of their relationships based on mutual consent and understanding, moving away from rigid templates that may not align with their authentic selves.

Moreover, changing attitudes toward marriage and cohabitation are reshaping the traditional trajectory of romantic relationships. The emphasis on personal growth, career aspirations, and individual well-being has led many individuals to delay or forgo marriage, focusing instead on building strong, fulfilling connections with their partners.

Redefining Gender Roles: Equality in Love and Partnership

One of the profound shifts in contemporary romantic relationships is the ongoing process of redefining traditional gender roles. The ideals of the past, where rigid expectations often dictated the roles of men and women in relationships, are giving way to a more egalitarian approach.

Modern couples increasingly prioritize equality and shared responsibilities in their relationships. The division of household chores, child-rearing duties, and financial responsibilities is becoming more balanced, reflecting a commitment to dismantling gender-based stereotypes.

The workplace, too, plays a crucial role in shaping the dynamics of romantic relationships. As gender equality gains traction in professional settings, couples are navigating dual-career households, addressing the challenges and opportunities that arise when both partners pursue ambitious careers.

The evolving understanding of gender fluidity further contributes to the transformation of relationship dynamics. Open conversations about gender identity and expression foster greater acceptance and inclusivity, allowing individuals to explore and express their authentic selves within the context of romantic partnerships.

Digital Communication and Intimacy: Navigating the Virtual Realm

The digital age has introduced novel dimensions to the way couples communicate and foster intimacy. The ubiquity of smartphones and the prevalence of social media platforms have created new channels for connection, but they also pose challenges to traditional notions of closeness and privacy.

Couples often engage in constant digital communication, exchanging messages, photos, and updates throughout the day. The digital realm provides a platform for expressing affection, sharing experiences, and maintaining a sense of closeness, especially for those in long-distance relationships.

However, the ease of digital communication also raises questions about the nature of intimacy in the virtual realm. Balancing the benefits of constant connectivity with the need for personal space and face-to-face interactions becomes a delicate task in modern relationships.

Relationships in the Age of Social Media: Sharing, Comparisons, and Privacy

The integration of social media into daily life has become a defining aspect of contemporary relationships. Couples navigate the challenges and opportunities presented by sharing their romantic journeys on public platforms, influencing how they present their partnerships to the world.

Social media offers a space for couples to share moments of joy, milestones, and expressions of love with a broad audience. However, the curated nature of social media often prompts individuals to present an idealized version of their relationships, raising questions about authenticity and the impact of external perceptions on the couple's dynamic.

The phenomenon of "relationship goals" propagated on social media platforms can create unrealistic expectations, leading to comparisons and potential feelings of inadequacy. The need to strike a balance between sharing meaningful aspects of a relationship and maintaining a sense of privacy becomes paramount in the age of digital transparency.

Impact of Time and Career Pressures: Balancing Love and Ambition

Contemporary romantic relationships often grapple with the demands of time and career pressures. The pursuit of ambitious careers, personal goals, and individual growth can create challenges in finding a harmonious balance between professional aspirations and romantic commitments.

Couples navigate the complexities of dual-career households, where both partners are actively engaged in their respective careers. The juggling act of balancing work responsibilities, personal aspirations, and relationship commitments requires effective communication, flexibility, and a shared understanding of priorities.

Time constraints, driven by hectic work schedules and external pressures, can affect the quality of time spent together. Couples may need to consciously carve out moments for connection, intimacy, and shared experiences to maintain a strong emotional bond amidst the challenges of a fast-paced, career-oriented lifestyle.

The Role of Empathy and Emotional Intelligence

In navigating the changing dynamics of romantic relationships, the role of empathy and emotional intelligence has become increasingly crucial. Couples are recognizing the significance of understanding and validating each other's emotions, fostering a deeper emotional connection that transcends traditional roles and expectations.

Empathy enables partners to navigate challenges, conflicts, and individual growth with a sense of understanding and compassion. Emotional intelligence, which involves recognizing, understanding, and managing one's own emotions as well as those of others, contributes to effective communication and conflict resolution within relationships.

The cultivation of empathy and emotional intelligence involves active listening, open communication, and a willingness to engage in vulnerability. Modern couples are embracing these qualities as essential tools for building resilient and fulfilling relationships in the face of evolving societal norms and expectations.

Cohabitation and Changing Notions of Commitment

The decision to cohabit before or instead of marriage has become a common aspect of contemporary romantic relationships. Cohabitation allows couples to test compatibility, share financial responsibilities, and gain insights into the practicalities of living together before making a formal commitment.

Changing societal attitudes toward cohabitation have led to a reevaluation of traditional notions of commitment. For some couples, cohabitation represents a significant step toward building a life together, with or without the formalization of marriage. This shift reflects a broader trend of redefining commitment based on individual preferences and relationship dynamics.

However, the decision to cohabit also comes with its own set of challenges, including the need for effective communication, shared responsibilities, and a clear understanding of each partner's expectations. Navigating the complexities of cohabitation requires a mutual commitment to transparency, compromise, and continuous growth within the relationship.

Conclusion: Embracing Change in Modern Love

The changing dynamics of romantic relationships in the contemporary era reflect a broader societal shift towards inclusivity, equality, and the recognition of diverse expressions of love. As couples navigate the complexities of modern romance, they are rewriting the script of traditional expectations, embracing the fluidity of gender roles, and incorporating technology into the fabric of their relationships.

In the subsequent chapters, we will delve into the influence of celebrity culture on Valentine's Day trends, the scientific perspectives on love, and the enduring legacy of Valentine's Day traditions. The exploration of these facets will contribute to a comprehensive understanding of how love continues to evolve and thrive across time and borders, shaped by the dynamic interplay of tradition, innovation, and individual agency.

Celebrity Influence on Valentine's Day Trends

In the age of social media and hyper-connectivity, the influence of celebrities extends far beyond the realms of entertainment and into the way we perceive, celebrate, and express love. Valentine's Day, as a cultural phenomenon, has not been immune to the impact of celebrity trends and public displays of affection. In this section, we delve into the ways in which celebrities shape Valentine's Day trends, influencing everything from romantic gestures to gift choices and relationship expectations.

Social Media as a Celebrity Love Platform

Celebrities often leverage the power of social media to share intimate moments of their romantic lives with the public. Platforms like Instagram, Twitter, and TikTok provide a direct line of communication between celebrities and their fans, offering a curated glimpse into their relationships.

Public declarations of love, romantic getaways, and carefully crafted images of thoughtful gestures become part of the celebrity narrative on Valentine's Day. The amplification of these moments through social media not only sets trends but also contributes to the construction of idealized notions of romance that permeate popular culture.

Influential Celebrity Couples: Setting Relationship Goals

Certain celebrity couples gain iconic status as relationship goals, shaping societal expectations and influencing Valentine's Day trends. The dynamics of power couples, such as Beyoncé and Jay-Z or David and Victoria Beckham, are often scrutinized and emulated.

The gestures and celebrations of these influential couples, whether it's a grand romantic gesture or a simple, heartfelt exchange, become benchmarks for fans seeking inspiration for their own relationships. The hashtag #RelationshipGoals often accompanies posts sharing glimpses of celebrity love, creating a virtual space where fans collectively celebrate and aspire to emulate these idealized notions of romance.

Celebrity-Endorsed Products and Experiences

Celebrities frequently collaborate with brands to create Valentine's Day-themed products or experiences. From signature fragrances and jewelry lines to curated gift boxes and exclusive experiences, these collaborations have a significant impact on consumer trends during the Valentine's Day season.

The association of a celebrity's image with a particular product or experience often results in increased consumer interest and sales. Fans, inspired by their favorite celebrities, may actively seek to incorporate these endorsed products into their own Valentine's Day celebrations, further driving trends in the gifting industry.

The Red Carpet Romance: Public Events and Award Shows

Valentine's Day often coincides with the awards season, providing celebrities with high-profile platforms to showcase their love. The red carpet becomes a stage for public displays of affection, with couples often posing for the cameras and sharing sweet moments that captivate audiences worldwide.

The fashion choices of celebrity couples, coordinated outfits, and joint appearances contribute to the creation of iconic images that are widely shared and celebrated. Fans may draw inspiration from these glamorous displays, influencing their own choices in attire and how they approach Valentine's Day celebrations.

Destination Celebrations: Influencing Travel Trends

Celebrity couples often choose picturesque and exotic locations for their Valentine's Day celebrations. The choice of a romantic getaway destination can influence travel trends as fans seek to recreate the magic experienced by their favorite celebrities.

Whether it's a secluded beach resort, a charming European city, or a cozy mountain retreat, the destinations chosen by celebrities for Valentine's Day celebrations contribute to the allure of specific locations as ideal romantic getaways. Travel agencies and hospitality services may see an uptick in bookings to these destinations as couples seek to replicate the experiences of their favorite stars.

Surprise Proposals and Grand Gestures

The trend of surprise proposals and grand romantic gestures on Valentine's Day is often heightened by the influence of celebrity culture. High-profile proposals, such as those at major events, during concerts, or on live television, capture the public's imagination and contribute to the notion of Valentine's Day as an ideal moment for grand declarations of love.

The expectation for elaborate proposals, often fueled by celebrity examples, has given rise to creative and extravagant ways individuals choose to pop the question on Valentine's Day. Social media platforms become flooded with videos and photos of unique proposals, further perpetuating the trend of larger-than-life romantic gestures.

Publicized Relationships and Media Scrutiny

The scrutiny of celebrity relationships by the media can have a profound impact on public perceptions of love and romance. Celebrity breakups and reconciliations become part of the narrative, influencing societal attitudes toward the transient nature of relationships.

The intense media focus on the romantic lives of celebrities, especially during the Valentine's Day season, can contribute to a heightened sense of pressure and expectations for individuals in their own relationships. The constant cycle of celebrity relationships entering the spotlight and facing scrutiny can shape public discourse around the challenges and complexities of modern love.

Celebrity Philanthropy and Social Causes on Valentine's Day

Some celebrities use Valentine's Day as an opportunity to promote philanthropy and support social causes. Publicizing charitable acts and encouraging fans to contribute to meaningful initiatives, celebrities leverage their influence to bring attention to issues such as humanitarian causes, environmental sustainability, and social justice.

Valentine's Day campaigns initiated by celebrities often involve fundraising, awareness-building, or direct participation in charitable events. The influence of these campaigns extends beyond traditional expressions of love to incorporate a broader sense of compassion and social responsibility.

Navigating the Dark Side: Celebrity Breakups and Heartbreak

While celebrity couples often showcase the idealized aspects of romance, the public also witnesses the challenges and heartbreaks when high-profile relationships come to an end. The media coverage of celebrity breakups, often accompanied by intense speculation and analysis, can contribute to a sense of disillusionment and skepticism about the durability of love.

The aftermath of celebrity breakups, played out in the public eye, may influence societal attitudes toward the transient nature of relationships. Fans may be prompted to reflect on the complexities of love and the challenges faced by individuals, regardless of their status or fame.

Conclusion: The Celebrity Tapestry of Valentine's Day

The influence of celebrities on Valentine's Day trends weaves a complex tapestry of inspiration, aspiration, and reflection. From the curated images of romance shared on social media to the high-stakes world of public events and red carpets, celebrities shape the cultural narrative around love and relationships.

As we explore the subsequent chapters on the science of love and the enduring legacy of Valentine's Day traditions, we will continue to unravel the intricate ways in which societal influences, both celebrity-driven and cultural, contribute to the ever-evolving landscape of modern love. The exploration of these facets will provide a comprehensive understanding of how love transcends borders and adapts to the dynamic interplay of tradition, innovation, and the pervasive influence of popular culture.

Virtual Celebrations and Long-Distance Love

In an era characterized by technological advancements and global connectivity, couples are redefining the boundaries of love and connection. Virtual celebrations and the ability to sustain long-distance relationships have become integral aspects of modern romance. This section explores the evolving dynamics of love in the digital age, where physical distance is no longer a barrier to celebrating special moments and maintaining meaningful connections.

The Rise of Virtual Celebrations

Virtual celebrations have become a cornerstone of modern relationships, allowing couples separated by distance to bridge the gap and share special moments in real-time. Whether it's a birthday, anniversary, or Valentine's Day, virtual celebrations enable couples to create shared experiences despite being physically apart.

Video conferencing platforms, such as Zoom, Skype, and FaceTime, have become the virtual venues for couples to celebrate together. These platforms facilitate face-to-face communication, allowing partners to see each other's expressions, share laughter, and create a sense of presence even when miles apart.

During Valentine's Day, virtual celebrations take on a romantic hue as couples exchange digital flowers, share virtual dinners, and even watch movies together through synchronized streaming. The creativity involved in planning and executing virtual celebrations adds a unique and personal touch to long-distance relationships.

Digital Gift Exchanges and Surprises

The digital landscape has expanded the possibilities for expressing love and thoughtfulness across distances. Couples engage in digital gift exchanges, sending e-cards, virtual flowers, and personalized messages to convey their affection. Online platforms offer a plethora of options for selecting and sending digital gifts that align with the recipient's preferences.

Virtual surprises, orchestrated with the help of friends, family, or online services, add an element of excitement to long-distance celebrations. From surprise video calls to virtual scavenger hunts leading to a special message, couples find innovative ways to create memorable and intimate moments despite the physical separation.

Digital subscriptions, such as streaming services, virtual book clubs, or online classes, provide opportunities for shared experiences. Couples can engage in activities together, even from afar, fostering a sense of connection and shared interests.

Celebrating Time Zone Challenges

One of the inherent challenges of long-distance relationships is navigating different time zones. Virtual celebrations require couples to coordinate schedules and find a time that suits both partners, taking into account potential delays or inconveniences.

Time zone challenges, however, also present opportunities for creativity. Some couples embrace the concept of a "24-Hour Valentine's Day," where celebrations unfold across different time zones, allowing each partner to plan surprises or share moments throughout the day.

Technology, such as world clocks and time zone converters, becomes an essential tool for couples managing the complexities of global time differences. Planning virtual celebrations with an understanding of time zone challenges adds an extra layer of thoughtfulness to long-distance relationships.

Virtual Dinner Dates and Culinary Connections

Sharing a meal is a traditional way for couples to connect, and technology has made it possible to extend this experience to virtual spaces. Virtual dinner dates allow couples to share a meal while being physically apart, creating a sense of togetherness even when separated by distance.

Couples may plan ahead to cook the same recipe or order from the same restaurant, creating a shared culinary experience. Video calls during the meal provide an opportunity for conversation, laughter, and a shared appreciation of food, transforming a simple dinner into a meaningful and romantic occasion.

Cooking together virtually also serves as a collaborative activity, reinforcing a sense of partnership and teamwork. The experience goes beyond the act of eating, becoming a way for couples to engage in a shared activity and create lasting memories.

Digital Scrapbooks and Shared Online Spaces

The digital realm offers opportunities for couples to create virtual scrapbooks and shared online spaces that document their journey and celebrate their love. Platforms like Google Drive, Dropbox, or dedicated apps for couples allow partners to compile photos, videos, and memories in a digital format.

Creating a digital scrapbook provides a collaborative and interactive way for couples to reminisce about shared experiences. It becomes a repository of cherished moments, from the first virtual date to special milestones celebrated online. The ability to access and contribute to the digital scrapbook enhances the sense of connection and shared history.

In addition to digital scrapbooks, couples may maintain shared playlists, collaborative documents, or joint social media accounts dedicated to their relationship. These shared online spaces become symbolic representations of the bond between partners, fostering a sense of unity and continuity.

Navigating the Emotional Challenges

While virtual celebrations and long-distance connections offer unique opportunities for maintaining relationships, they also come with emotional challenges. The absence of physical proximity can lead to feelings of loneliness, longing, and frustration. Navigating these emotions requires open communication, trust, and a commitment to the shared goals of the relationship.

Couples in long-distance relationships often experience a heightened need for effective communication. Regular video calls, voice messages, and text exchanges become essential tools for staying connected. Establishing routines for communication helps create a sense of predictability and reliability in the relationship.

The challenges of long-distance love may also include managing jealousy and insecurity. The digital age introduces new dynamics, such as navigating social media interactions and the potential for misunderstandings. Couples must actively address these concerns through transparent communication and a mutual understanding of boundaries.

Celebrating milestones virtually can also bring a mix of emotions. While technology enables couples to share special moments, the absence of physical presence may intensify the desire for closeness. Balancing the joy of celebration with the longing for physical connection requires emotional resilience and a shared commitment to the future.

Innovations in Virtual Reality (VR) and Augmented Reality (AR)

As technology continues to advance, innovations in virtual reality (VR) and augmented reality (AR) offer new possibilities for enhancing virtual experiences in long-distance relationships. VR allows couples to create immersive environments where they can virtually spend time together, explore digital landscapes, or attend virtual events.

AR applications can overlay digital elements onto the real world, offering creative ways to enhance virtual celebrations. From sending virtual flowers that appear in the recipient's physical space to creating digital surprises visible through smartphones, AR adds an extra layer of interactivity and personalization to long-distance connections.

While these technologies are still evolving, they represent exciting prospects for the future of virtual celebrations and long-distance relationships. As VR and AR become more accessible, couples may find increasingly innovative ways to bridge the physical gap and create shared experiences in digital spaces.

Conclusion: Love Beyond Borders and Screens

Virtual celebrations and long-distance love have become integral components of the modern romantic landscape, transcending geographical boundaries and bringing couples closer in the digital realm. As we explore the subsequent chapters, delving into the scientific perspectives on love and the enduring legacy of Valentine's Day traditions, we will continue to unravel the intricate ways in which love evolves and thrives across time and borders, shaped by the dynamic interplay of tradition, innovation, and the resilient spirit of human connection.

Chapter 7: The Science of Love
The Psychology of Love

Love, a complex and multifaceted emotion, has intrigued scholars, poets, and thinkers throughout history. In the realm of psychology, understanding the intricacies of love involves exploring cognitive, emotional, and behavioral aspects that contribute to the human experience of this powerful emotion. This section delves into the psychological dimensions of love, examining the theories, mechanisms, and factors that shape how individuals perceive, experience, and express love.

Defining Love: A Multifaceted Emotion

Psychologists acknowledge that love is a complex and multi-dimensional emotion, encompassing various forms and expressions. Robert Sternberg's Triangular Theory of Love posits that love consists of three components: intimacy, passion, and commitment. Different combinations of these components give rise to distinct types of love, such as romantic love, companionate love, and consummate love.

Additionally, psychologist Elaine Hatfield proposed the Two-Factor Theory of Love, emphasizing both passionate or romantic love and companionate love. The interplay between these two dimensions contributes to the richness and diversity of the emotional landscape of love.

Psychological perspectives also highlight cultural variations in the conceptualization and expression of love. The ways in which love is defined and experienced can be influenced by cultural norms, societal expectations, and individual beliefs, adding layers of complexity to the psychology of love.

Theories of Love: Exploring the Landscape

Numerous psychological theories have been developed to unravel the mysteries of love, each offering a unique lens through which to understand this intricate emotion.

1. Attachment Theory: Developed by John Bowlby and Mary Ainsworth, attachment theory explores the impact of early caregiver relationships on later romantic attachments. Secure attachment in childhood is linked to healthier and more secure adult relationships, while insecure attachment may contribute to relationship challenges.

2. Social Exchange Theory: This theory, rooted in the work of sociologist George Homans, suggests that individuals seek relationships that maximize rewards and minimize costs. The perceived value of a relationship influences feelings of love and commitment.

3. Evolutionary Psychology: Drawing on principles of natural selection, evolutionary psychology posits that certain behaviors associated with love, such as mate selection and pair bonding, have evolved to enhance the chances of reproductive success. This perspective explores how biological factors contribute to human mating strategies.

4. Cognitive Theories: Cognitive theories of love, including those proposed by Zick Rubin and Robert J. Sternberg, emphasize the cognitive processes involved in forming and maintaining loving relationships. These theories explore factors such as perception, judgment, and decision-making in the context of romantic connections.

The Tripartite Model of Love: Sternberg's Contribution

Robert J. Sternberg's Triangular Theory of Love is a prominent framework that classifies love into three components:

1. Intimacy: Refers to feelings of closeness, connection, and emotional support in a relationship. Intimate bonds involve sharing thoughts, feelings, and personal experiences with a partner.

2. Passion: Encompasses the physical and emotional intensity of romantic attraction. Passionate love involves desire, arousal, and a strong emotional connection characterized by infatuation.

3. Commitment: Involves the decision to maintain a long-term relationship and work towards its future. Commitment includes elements of stability, dedication, and the intention to endure challenges together.

Sternberg's model suggests that various combinations of these components give rise to different types of love:

- Romantic Love: High in both intimacy and passion, romantic love is characterized by strong emotional bonds and physical attraction. It often marks the early stages of a romantic relationship.

- Companionate Love: High in intimacy and commitment, companionate love is associated with deep emotional connections and a long-term commitment. While passionate intensity may diminish, the relationship is characterized by friendship and mutual support.

- Consummate Love: Involves high levels of intimacy, passion, and commitment. Consummate love represents an ideal state characterized by enduring passion, deep emotional connection, and a sustained commitment to the relationship.

Sternberg's model provides a comprehensive framework for understanding the dynamic nature of love and how it evolves over time in relationships.

Attachment Theory: The Foundation of Emotional Bonds

Attachment theory, initially developed by John Bowlby and expanded by Mary Ainsworth, focuses on the impact of early caregiver relationships on the formation of emotional bonds and adult romantic attachments.

- Secure Attachment: Individuals with a secure attachment style tend to form healthy and secure relationships. They feel comfortable with emotional intimacy, trust their partners, and are generally confident in the stability of their relationships.

- Anxious Attachment: Those with an anxious attachment style may experience fears of abandonment and seek reassurance and closeness in relationships. They may be more sensitive to perceived threats to the relationship's stability.

- Avoidant Attachment: Individuals with an avoidant attachment style may exhibit discomfort with emotional intimacy and may prioritize independence and self-sufficiency. They may struggle with closeness and may be hesitant to fully engage in romantic relationships.

Attachment styles established in childhood can influence adult romantic relationships. Partners with compatible attachment styles often experience smoother and more satisfying connections, while mismatched attachment styles may lead to challenges in communication and emotional responsiveness.

Love and the Brain: A Neurobiological Perspective

Neurobiological research has provided insights into the brain processes associated with love, shedding light on the chemical and neural mechanisms that underlie romantic emotions.

- Oxytocin and Vasopressin: Often referred to as the "love hormones," oxytocin and vasopressin play crucial roles in bonding and attachment. These hormones are released during intimate moments, contributing to feelings of trust, bonding, and emotional connection.

- Dopamine and Reward Pathways: Romantic love is associated with increased dopamine levels in the brain's reward pathways. Dopamine, a neurotransmitter linked to pleasure and reward, is released during activities associated with love, contributing to the feelings of joy and motivation.

- Serotonin and Mood Regulation: Serotonin, a neurotransmitter linked to mood regulation, may also play a role in love. The fluctuation of serotonin levels may contribute to the emotional highs and lows experienced in romantic relationships.

- Brain Imaging Studies: Functional magnetic resonance imaging (fMRI) studies have provided visual representations of brain activity during experiences of love. Areas of the brain associated with reward, pleasure, and emotional processing, such as the ventral tegmental area (VTA) and the caudate nucleus, show heightened activity during romantic love.

Understanding the neurobiological basis of love highlights the intricate interplay between brain chemistry and emotional experiences, contributing to a more comprehensive understanding of the psychology of love.

Cultural and Societal Influences on Love

While psychological theories provide frameworks for understanding love at an individual level, cultural and societal influences shape the broader context in which love is conceptualized and expressed.

- Cultural Variations in Expressions of Love: Different cultures may have distinct norms and expectations regarding how love is expressed. The emphasis on individual autonomy versus collective harmony, the role of arranged marriages, and cultural rituals surrounding courtship all contribute to diverse manifestations of love.

- Societal Expectations and Relationship Norms: Societal expectations regarding romantic relationships can influence individual perceptions and behaviors. Expectations regarding gender roles, relationship milestones, and societal attitudes toward various forms of love, including non-traditional relationships, contribute to the social context in which love unfolds.

- Media and Popular Culture: Media representations, including literature, films, and music, play a significant role in shaping societal perceptions of love. Romantic narratives presented in popular culture contribute to idealized notions of love and influence individuals' expectations and aspirations in their own relationships.

- Changing Definitions of Love: Societal attitudes toward love are dynamic and subject to change over time. Shifts in societal values, evolving gender roles, and changing family structures contribute to the redefinition of love in contemporary contexts.

Understanding the interplay between individual psychological processes and broader cultural and societal influences provides a nuanced perspective on the complexities of love as a universal yet culturally embedded phenomenon.

Love Languages: Understanding Expression and Communication

Psychologist Gary Chapman introduced the concept of love languages, proposing that individuals have distinct ways of expressing and receiving love. The five love languages are:

1. Words of Affirmation: Expressing love through verbal affirmations, compliments, and words of encouragement.

2. Acts of Service: Demonstrating love through helpful actions and gestures that alleviate the burden on a partner.

3. Receiving Gifts: Communicating love through thoughtful and meaningful gifts that convey appreciation and care.

4. Quality Time: Prioritizing and dedicating undivided attention to a partner, creating moments of shared connection.

5. Physical Touch: Expressing love through physical affection, such as hugs, kisses, and other forms of touch.

Understanding one's own love language and that of a partner can enhance communication and foster a deeper emotional connection. Couples who are attuned to each other's love languages can express love in ways that resonate most profoundly with their partner's preferences.

The Dark Side of Love: Obsessive Love and Unhealthy Attachments

While love is generally considered a positive and fulfilling emotion, it can sometimes manifest in unhealthy and obsessive forms. Obsessive love, characterized by an intense and intrusive preoccupation with a partner, may lead to negative outcomes for both individuals involved.

- Obsessive Love Scale: Researchers have developed the Obsessive Love Scale to measure the degree of obsession in romantic relationships. High scores on the scale may indicate problematic patterns of intrusive thoughts, possessiveness, and an inability to tolerate separation.

- Unhealthy Attachments: Unhealthy attachments may involve a disproportionate reliance on a partner for emotional well-being, fear of abandonment, and difficulty maintaining a sense of self outside the relationship. Such attachments can lead to codependency and emotional distress.

- Jealousy and Possessiveness: Excessive jealousy and possessiveness are common manifestations of obsessive love. Unfounded suspicions, controlling behaviors, and attempts to limit a partner's autonomy can contribute to relationship conflicts and distress.

Understanding the signs of obsessive love is crucial for maintaining healthy relationships. Psychoeducation, counseling, and interventions focused on enhancing communication and emotional regulation can be beneficial for individuals experiencing or exhibiting patterns of obsessive love.

Conclusion: A Tapestry of Psychological Love

The psychology of love is a rich and intricate tapestry woven from threads of emotion, cognition, behavior, and neurobiology. As we explore the subsequent chapters, unraveling the legacy of Valentine's Day traditions and envisioning the future of love, we will continue to deepen our understanding of how psychological processes contribute to the ever-evolving landscape of human connection. The journey through the science of love invites us to explore the depths of our emotions, the complexities of our relationships, and the profound ways in which love shapes the human experience.

Biological Basis of Romance

Romance, a captivating and emotionally charged aspect of human relationships, finds its roots in the intricate interplay of biological processes. Understanding the biological basis of romance delves into the neurochemical, hormonal, and genetic mechanisms that contribute to the experience of romantic attraction, bonding, and attachment. This section explores how biology shapes the landscape of romance, providing insights into the physiological underpinnings of love.

Neurochemical Orchestra: The Role of Brain Chemicals in Romance

Romantic love is orchestrated by a symphony of neurochemicals that influence mood, motivation, and bonding. These chemicals create a cascade of sensations and emotions, contributing to the euphoria and intensity associated with being in love.

- Dopamine: Often referred to as the "feel-good" neurotransmitter, dopamine is central to the experience of pleasure and reward. In the context of romance, dopamine levels surge during moments of attraction, infatuation, and anticipation of being with a loved one. This surge creates a sense of excitement and motivation, reinforcing the desire to pursue and connect with a romantic partner.

- Oxytocin: Commonly known as the "love hormone" or "bonding hormone," oxytocin plays a crucial role in social bonding and attachment. Released in response to physical touch, intimate contact, and positive social interactions, oxytocin fosters feelings of trust, closeness, and emotional connection. The release of oxytocin is particularly pronounced during activities such as hugging, kissing, and cuddling.

- Serotonin: Serotonin, a neurotransmitter linked to mood regulation, also plays a role in romantic love. Fluctuations in serotonin levels contribute to the emotional highs and lows associated with being in love. The initial stages of romantic attraction are often characterized by elevated serotonin, contributing to feelings of happiness and excitement.

- Endorphins: Endorphins, the body's natural painkillers and mood enhancers, are released during pleasurable activities. In the context of romance, endorphins contribute to the overall sense of well-being and happiness experienced when in the presence of a loved one.

- Adrenaline (Epinephrine): The "fight or flight" hormone, adrenaline, is also involved in the experience of romantic love. During moments of excitement, such as the thrill of a new relationship or the anticipation of seeing a loved one, adrenaline levels increase, contributing to heightened arousal and energy.

The intricate dance of these neurochemicals creates a biochemical backdrop for the emotional highs and intense connection associated with romantic love.

Hormonal Influences on Romance: The Love Hormones

Hormones, chemical messengers produced by the endocrine system, play a vital role in regulating various physiological processes, including those related to romance.

- Testosterone: Often associated with libido and sexual desire, testosterone also influences romantic attraction and behavior. Research suggests that increased testosterone levels in both men and women may enhance feelings of confidence, assertiveness, and the motivation to pursue romantic interests.

- Estrogen: While estrogen is traditionally linked to female reproductive health, it also contributes to mood regulation and the perception of attractiveness. Fluctuations in estrogen levels, particularly during the menstrual cycle, can influence how individuals perceive and respond to potential romantic partners.

- Prolactin: Released after orgasm, prolactin is involved in promoting feelings of relaxation and contentment. While traditionally associated with lactation, prolactin's role in the post-sexual experience contributes to the emotional bonding between partners.

- Vasopressin: Alongside oxytocin, vasopressin is a key hormone in the formation of social bonds and attachment. Vasopressin is associated with mate guarding behavior and the desire for emotional closeness with a romantic partner. Studies have linked variations in the vasopressin receptor gene to relationship satisfaction and bonding patterns.

Understanding the hormonal influences on romance provides a deeper appreciation for the biological mechanisms that contribute to the complex and nuanced experience of love.

Genetics of Attraction: The Love Blueprint in Our DNA

Genetics, the study of inherited traits and genetic variation, also plays a role in shaping romantic attraction and compatibility.

- Major Histocompatibility Complex (MHC): Research suggests that individuals may be attracted to partners with a different MHC, a set of genes involved in the immune system. This phenomenon, known as the "sweaty T-shirt experiment," proposes that people are drawn to the natural scent of individuals with a complementary MHC, possibly contributing to genetic diversity in offspring.

- Dopamine Receptor Genes: Variations in genes related to dopamine receptors may influence individual differences in the experience of romantic love. Some studies suggest that specific genetic variations may be associated with relationship satisfaction, infidelity, and the intensity of romantic feelings.

- Oxytocin Receptor Gene: Genetic variations in the oxytocin receptor gene have been linked to differences in social behavior, attachment styles, and relationship satisfaction. Individuals with certain variations may exhibit heightened sensitivity to oxytocin, influencing their emotional responses in romantic relationships.

- Serotonin Transporter Gene: Genetic variations in the serotonin transporter gene may contribute to differences in emotional regulation and susceptibility to mood disorders. These genetic factors can influence how individuals navigate the emotional complexities of romantic love.

While genetics provides a blueprint, it's essential to recognize the interaction between genes and the environment. Environmental factors, life experiences, and personal choices also contribute to the development and expression of romantic relationships.

The Evolutionary Perspective: Love as an Adaptive Mechanism

From an evolutionary standpoint, love is considered an adaptive mechanism that contributes to the survival and reproduction of the species. Evolutionary psychology explores how behaviors and traits related to love may have evolved to enhance the chances of reproductive success.

- Mate Selection: Evolutionary theories propose that mate selection is influenced by factors such as physical attractiveness, fertility, and indicators of genetic fitness. Preferences for certain traits, such as facial symmetry and waist-to-hip ratio, may be rooted in evolutionary mechanisms that signal reproductive health.

- Parental Investment Theory: Developed by Robert Trivers, the parental investment theory posits that the sex that invests more in offspring (typically females) is more selective in mate choice, while the sex with lower investment (typically males) competes for mating opportunities. This theory provides insights into mating strategies, preferences, and behaviors.

- Attachment and Bonding: Attachment behaviors, such as the bond between caregivers and offspring, are considered adaptive mechanisms that promote the survival and well-being of dependent offspring. The attachment system extends to adult romantic relationships, influencing bonding and relationship dynamics.

- Intrasexual Competition: Intrasexual competition, where members of the same sex compete for access to mates, is a concept explored in evolutionary psychology. Competitive behaviors, such as displays of physical prowess or resources, may be rooted in adaptive strategies for securing mating opportunities.

The evolutionary perspective on love highlights the role of biological mechanisms in shaping human mating strategies, partner preferences, and relationship dynamics.

The Role of Physical Attractiveness: Evolutionary and Cultural Influences

Physical attractiveness is a key component of romantic attraction, influenced by both evolutionary and cultural factors.

- Evolutionary Influences: Evolutionary theories propose that preferences for certain physical traits are linked to indicators of reproductive fitness. Features such as facial symmetry, clear skin, and indicators of health may signal genetic quality and fertility, influencing mate selection.

- Cultural Influences: Cultural ideals of beauty and attractiveness vary across societies and time periods. While some features may have universal appeal due to evolutionary factors, cultural standards also play a significant role in shaping perceptions of attractiveness. Cultural variations in beauty standards may include preferences for body size, facial features, and grooming practices.

- Media and Beauty Standards: Media representations, including advertising, films, and social media, contribute to the dissemination of cultural beauty ideals. The portrayal of idealized images in media can influence individual self-perception and societal expectations regarding physical attractiveness.

- Attractiveness and Relationship Dynamics: Physical attractiveness can influence initial impressions, mate selection, and relationship satisfaction. Research suggests that physically attractive individuals may be perceived as more socially competent, leading to advantages in social interactions and relationship formation.

Understanding the interplay between evolutionary preferences and cultural influences provides a nuanced perspective on the role of physical attractiveness in romantic relationships.

Love, Sexuality, and the Brain: Exploring the Neurobiology of Intimacy

The neurobiology of intimacy involves examining how the brain processes and responds to sexual experiences, bonding, and the emotional dimensions of physical intimacy.

- The Sexual Response Cycle: The sexual response cycle, proposed by William Masters and Virginia Johnson, includes phases of excitement, plateau, orgasm, and resolution. Each phase involves distinct neurobiological processes, including changes in blood flow, hormone release, and neurotransmitter activity.

- Hormonal Changes During Sex: Sexual activity triggers the release of various hormones, including oxytocin and endorphins. These hormones contribute to feelings of pleasure, emotional bonding, and relaxation.

- Brain Regions Involved in Sexual Response: The brain regions involved in sexual response include the hypothalamus, amygdala, and prefrontal cortex. These areas play roles in regulating sexual arousal, emotional processing, and decision-making related to sexual behavior.

- The Role of Dopamine in Sexual Reward: Dopamine, a neurotransmitter associated with reward and pleasure, plays a significant role in the sexual reward system. Dopaminergic pathways are activated during sexual arousal and orgasm, contributing to the pleasurable sensations associated with sexual experiences.

- Attachment and Intimacy: The neurobiology of intimacy extends beyond sexual activity to include the bonding and attachment processes associated with emotional connection. Oxytocin, released during intimate moments, fosters emotional closeness and bonding between partners.

Love and Aging: How Relationships Evolve Over Time

The dynamics of romantic love evolve over the course of a relationship, influenced by factors such as aging, life experiences, and changes in individual and relational priorities.

- Long-Term Relationship Changes: Research suggests that the intensity of romantic love may evolve in long-term relationships. While the initial stages of a relationship may be marked by passionate love, the dynamics may transition to companionate love characterized by deep emotional connection, shared experiences, and mutual support.

- Neurobiological Changes: Aging is associated with neurobiological changes that can influence romantic relationships. Hormonal fluctuations, changes in neurotransmitter activity, and alterations in brain structure may contribute to shifts in emotional regulation, sexual response, and attachment dynamics.

- The Impact of Life Experiences: Life experiences, such as parenthood, career changes, and health challenges, can influence relationship dynamics. Navigating these experiences together can deepen emotional bonds and resilience within a partnership.

- Adaptation and Resilience: The ability of individuals and couples to adapt to changes and challenges is crucial for the long-term success of romantic relationships. Resilience, effective communication, and mutual support contribute to the enduring nature of love over time.

Understanding the neurobiological foundations of love provides a holistic perspective on the intricate interplay between biology, emotion, and behavior in romantic relationships. As we continue our exploration of the science of love, we will further unravel the complexities of human connection and the enduring legacy of romantic traditions.

Love and the Brain: A Scientific Perspective

The intricate dance of love, that sublime and often elusive emotion, finds its roots in the complex symphony of the human brain. As we embark on a scientific exploration of love and the brain, we delve into the neural intricacies that underlie the experience of this powerful emotion. From the firing of neurons to the release of neurotransmitters, the brain orchestrates the symphony of love in a manner that transcends cultural, temporal, and individual boundaries.

The Neuroscience of Attraction: The Initial Spark

The journey of love often begins with attraction—an intricate interplay of visual, olfactory, and auditory stimuli that trigger a cascade of neural responses.

- Visual Processing: The brain's visual processing centers, such as the occipital lobe, play a crucial role in perceiving and assessing physical attractiveness. Studies have shown that symmetrical facial features, clear skin, and other indicators of health and genetic fitness are processed as attractive by the brain.

- Olfactory Perception: The olfactory system, connected to the limbic system (the emotional center of the brain), contributes to the assessment of a potential partner's pheromones. Pheromones, chemical signals released by the body, may influence attraction and mate selection, contributing to the instinctual aspects of human attraction.

- Auditory Cues: The auditory processing centers in the brain contribute to the assessment of voice pitch, tone, and other vocal characteristics. Research suggests that certain vocal qualities are perceived as more attractive and may influence initial impressions.

The Role of the Limbic System: Love's Emotional Center

The limbic system, often referred to as the "emotional brain," plays a central role in processing and regulating emotions, including those associated with love.

- The Amygdala: The amygdala, a key component of the limbic system, is involved in the processing of emotional stimuli, including those related to attraction, fear, and pleasure. In the context of love, the amygdala responds to emotionally charged cues and contributes to the emotional coloring of romantic experiences.

- The Hippocampus: The hippocampus, another limbic structure, is associated with memory formation and consolidation. In the context of love, the hippocampus plays a role in encoding and retrieving memories of romantic experiences, contributing to the establishment of emotional bonds.

- The Hypothalamus: The hypothalamus is a crucial hub in the regulation of physiological processes, including those related to stress, reward, and sexual arousal. It plays a role in coordinating the body's response to emotional and physical aspects of love.

Neurotransmitters and Love: The Chemistry of Connection

Love is not only an emotional experience but also a biochemical one, with neurotransmitters acting as messengers that facilitate communication between neurons.

- Dopamine: Often referred to as the "reward neurotransmitter," dopamine is central to the experience of pleasure and motivation. In the context of love, dopamine is released during rewarding experiences, such as spending time with a loved one. This surge of dopamine contributes to the feelings of joy, excitement, and anticipation associated with love.

- Oxytocin: Known as the "love hormone" or "bonding hormone," oxytocin plays a crucial role in social bonding, attachment, and trust. Released during activities such as hugging, kissing, and physical touch, oxytocin fosters emotional closeness and deepens the connection between individuals in romantic relationships.

- Serotonin: Serotonin, a neurotransmitter associated with mood regulation, also influences the experience of love. Fluctuations in serotonin levels may contribute to the emotional highs and lows associated with romantic attraction and attachment.

- Endorphins: Endorphins, the body's natural painkillers and mood enhancers, are released during pleasurable activities. In the context of love, endorphins contribute to the overall sense of well-being and happiness experienced when in the presence of a loved one.

The Ventral Tegmental Area (VTA) and Romantic Reward

At the heart of the brain's reward system is the ventral tegmental area (VTA), a region associated with pleasure and motivation. The VTA plays a pivotal role in the experience of romantic love, responding to stimuli associated with a loved one and reinforcing the desire to seek and maintain connection.

- Activation During Romantic Attraction: Neuroimaging studies have shown increased activity in the VTA during the early stages of romantic attraction. The VTA responds to cues such as the sight or thought of a loved one, contributing to the feelings of euphoria and motivation to pursue the relationship.

- Association with Dopamine Release: The VTA is a primary source of dopamine release in the brain. The dopamine pathways originating in the VTA and projecting to other brain regions contribute to the reward and reinforcement associated with romantic love.

Attachment and the Striatum: Forming Emotional Bonds

The striatum, a part of the brain involved in reward processing and motor function, plays a crucial role in forming and maintaining emotional bonds in romantic relationships.

- Reward Processing: The striatum is implicated in the brain's reward circuitry, responding to stimuli associated with pleasure and reinforcement. In the context of love, the striatum responds to the presence and actions of a loved one, contributing to the positive reinforcement of the relationship.

- Oxytocin's Influence: Oxytocin, released during moments of intimacy and connection, enhances the activation of the striatum. This amplification of reward signals reinforces the emotional bonds formed during romantic interactions.

The Prefrontal Cortex: Love's Executive Director

The prefrontal cortex, the brain's executive control center, plays a crucial role in regulating and modulating the emotional and behavioral aspects of love.

- Decision-Making in Love: The prefrontal cortex is involved in decision-making, weighing the pros and cons of actions and choices related to love. It contributes to the evaluation of long-term compatibility, the assessment of relationship satisfaction, and the management of conflicts.

- Inhibition of Impulsive Behaviors: Love, with its intense emotions and desires, can elicit impulsive behaviors. The prefrontal cortex acts as a regulatory force, inhibiting impulsive actions and promoting thoughtful and reasoned responses in the context of love.

Love and the Aging Brain: Navigating Changes Over Time

As relationships evolve over time, the aging brain undergoes changes that influence the dynamics of romantic love.

- Neuroplasticity and Adaptation: The brain exhibits neuroplasticity, the ability to reorganize and adapt. Long-term romantic relationships can lead to changes in neural circuits associated with love and attachment, reflecting the adaptation to shared experiences and the development of emotional closeness.

- Hormonal Changes: Aging is associated with hormonal changes that can influence the experience of love. Fluctuations in hormone levels, including oxytocin and testosterone, may contribute to shifts in emotional and sexual aspects of romantic relationships.

- Cognitive Changes: Age-related changes in cognitive functions, such as memory and executive control, can influence how individuals perceive and navigate love. The ability to recall and reflect on shared experiences becomes a crucial aspect of maintaining emotional bonds.

Cultural and Individual Variations in Love's Neural Expression

While there are universal aspects to the neural basis of love, cultural and individual variations contribute to the diversity of romantic experiences.

- Cultural Influences: Cultural norms, values, and relationship expectations shape the expression of love and influence the neural processing of romantic stimuli. Variations in cultural practices, such as norms regarding physical affection or the role of arranged marriages, contribute to differences in the neural experience of love.

- Individual Differences: Each individual brings a unique set of experiences, personality traits, and attachment styles to their experience of love. These individual differences influence how the brain processes and responds to romantic stimuli, contributing to the diversity of love experiences.

The Dark Side of Love: Neuroscience of Heartbreak and Loss

Love's journey is not without its challenges, and the neuroscience of heartbreak sheds light on the emotional and neural processes associated with the dissolution of romantic relationships.

- Brain Regions Involved in Heartbreak: Neuroimaging studies have identified brain regions associated with the experience of heartbreak, including the anterior cingulate cortex and the insula. These regions are involved in processing emotional pain and social rejection.

- Neurotransmitter Changes: The end of a romantic relationship can lead to changes in neurotransmitter activity, including alterations in dopamine and serotonin levels. These changes contribute to the emotional distress and mood fluctuations associated with heartbreak.

- Overlap with Addiction Circuitry: The neural processes associated with heartbreak exhibit similarities to the brain circuitry involved in addiction. The withdrawal symptoms and craving for the presence of a former partner parallel the neurological patterns observed in substance dependence.

The Future of Love: Neurotechnological Explorations

Advancements in neurotechnology offer intriguing possibilities for exploring and enhancing the neural basis of love.

- Neuroimaging and Love Research: Continued advancements in neuroimaging techniques, such as functional magnetic resonance imaging (fMRI) and electroencephalography (EEG), provide researchers with unprecedented insights into the real-time neural processes associated with love. These technologies offer the potential to deepen our understanding of the temporal dynamics of love experiences.

- Neurofeedback and Emotional Regulation: Neurofeedback, a technique that allows individuals to observe and modulate their own brain activity, holds promise for enhancing emotional regulation in the context of love. This technology could offer tools for individuals and couples to navigate emotional challenges and enhance relationship well-being.

- Neural Interfaces and Connection: Emerging technologies, including neural interfaces, raise questions about the potential for enhancing interpersonal connection at the neural level. While these possibilities pose ethical considerations, they also open new avenues for exploring the intersection of technology and love.

Conclusion: The Infinite Landscape of Love in the Brain

As we navigate the neural landscape of love, we encounter a terrain rich in complexity, diversity, and adaptability. From the initial spark of attraction to the enduring bonds formed over time, the brain's orchestration of love reflects the profound interplay between biology, emotion, and cognition. The scientific exploration of love's neural basis invites us to contemplate the infinite variations of human connection, the universal threads that bind us, and the potential for continued discoveries in the ever-evolving field of neuroscience.

Cultural and Societal Influences on Love

Love, that intricate tapestry of emotions and connections, is woven into the fabric of cultural and societal norms. As we unravel the scientific exploration of love, it becomes imperative to understand how cultural and societal influences shape the expression, perception, and experience of this universal phenomenon. Love is not only a personal journey but also a collective narrative influenced by the rich tapestry of traditions, values, and expectations woven by societies across time and geography.

Cultural Constructs of Love: Diverse Expressions Across Societies

Love is not a monolithic concept; its definition and expression vary across cultures. Cultural constructs influence how individuals conceptualize love, the expectations surrounding romantic relationships, and the rituals that mark significant milestones.

- Arranged Marriages: In many cultures, arranged marriages have been a longstanding tradition, with families playing a pivotal role in match-making. The emphasis often lies on compatibility, family values, and shared socio-economic backgrounds rather than solely on individual feelings of love. Over time, these unions may evolve into deep, affectionate relationships.

- Romantic Love Ideals: In Western societies, the notion of romantic love as the foundation for marriage gained prominence, especially during the Romantic era. The emphasis on personal choice, emotional connection, and passion became central to the cultural narrative of love. However, variations exist even within Western cultures, with differences in attitudes toward dating, courtship, and marital expectations.

- Collective vs. Individual Focus: Some cultures prioritize the collective well-being and familial harmony over individual desires. In contrast, others emphasize individual autonomy and personal fulfillment in romantic relationships. These cultural variations influence relationship dynamics, decision-making processes, and the perceived role of love in one's life.

Cultural Rituals and Traditions: Ceremonies of Love

Cultural rituals and traditions play a significant role in the celebration and expression of love. These ceremonies not only mark milestones in romantic relationships but also contribute to the cultural continuity of love narratives.

- Wedding Ceremonies: Wedding ceremonies, with their diverse customs, symbolize the union of two individuals and their families. Whether it's the exchange of vows, the wearing of specific attire, or the participation in symbolic rituals, weddings reflect cultural values and expectations related to love and commitment.

- Festivals Celebrating Love: Across the world, various festivals are dedicated to the celebration of love. From the vibrant colors of Holi in India to the romantic traditions of Tanabata in Japan, these cultural festivals contribute to the collective expression of love within societies.

- Rites of Passage: Cultural rites of passage, such as engagement ceremonies, coming-of-age rituals, or anniversaries, mark significant stages in romantic relationships. These rituals reinforce the cultural significance of love and commitment, providing a framework for expressing and celebrating these emotions.

Love in Religion: Spiritual Dimensions of Connection

Religious beliefs often intertwine with cultural perspectives on love, adding a spiritual dimension to romantic relationships. The teachings, values, and moral guidelines provided by religious traditions influence how individuals perceive love, commitment, and the purpose of romantic unions.

- Sacred Unions: Many religious traditions sanctify the bond between partners, considering it a sacred union. Marriage ceremonies often involve religious rites, blessings, or sacraments that emphasize the divine nature of love and the spiritual connection between spouses.

- Moral and Ethical Guidelines: Religious teachings often provide moral and ethical guidelines for love and relationships. These guidelines may influence aspects such as premarital relationships, fidelity, and the role of love in family life. The intersection of religious and cultural values shapes the moral landscape within which love is cultivated and expressed.

- Love as a Virtue: In several religious traditions, love is regarded as a virtuous quality. Whether it's the Christian concept of agape, the Islamic emphasis on compassion, or the Hindu idea of divine love, religious teachings encourage the cultivation of love as a moral and spiritual virtue.

Societal Expectations and Pressures: Navigating the Landscape of Love

Societal expectations, norms, and pressures contribute to the shaping of individual and collective narratives around love. These societal influences create a framework within which individuals navigate the complexities of romantic relationships.

- Gender Roles and Love: Societal expectations regarding gender roles often impact the dynamics of romantic relationships. Cultural norms may prescribe specific roles, responsibilities, and behaviors for men and women in love, influencing how individuals express affection and navigate relationship dynamics.

- Family and Community Involvement: Many societies place significant importance on the involvement of families and communities in romantic relationships. The support or scrutiny of extended networks can impact decisions related to marriage, raising questions about autonomy, interdependence, and the role of the broader social context in individual love stories.

- Social Stigma and Acceptance: Societal attitudes toward diverse expressions of love, including LGBTQ+ relationships, can vary widely. While some societies embrace and celebrate these relationships, others may harbor stigma or discrimination. Negotiating societal acceptance and navigating the intersection of personal and societal values becomes a part of the love journey.

Love in Literature and Arts: Cultural Reflections

Literature, arts, and cultural expressions serve as mirrors reflecting the sentiments, ideals, and complexities of love within a society. From ancient epics to modern novels, cultural artifacts shape and are shaped by the evolving narrative of love.

- Love in Mythology and Folklore: Myths and folklore often weave tales of love that capture cultural values and archetypal symbols. These stories, passed down through generations, contribute to the cultural understanding of love and its various facets.

- Romanticism in Arts: The Romantic era in literature and arts, spanning the late 18th to mid-19th centuries, elevated the celebration of love, emotion, and nature. Romantic poets, painters, and composers expressed the intensity of love and longing, leaving an indelible mark on cultural perceptions of romance.

- Cultural Love Epics: Many cultures boast love epics or stories that have become cultural touchstones. Whether it's the epic of Layla and Majnun in Islamic literature, the tales of Krishna and Radha in Hindu mythology, or the tragic love stories in Shakespearean plays, these narratives resonate with cultural values and themes.

Globalization and Cultural Exchange: Shaping Love in a Connected World

In the contemporary era, globalization has led to increased cultural exchange, influencing how love is perceived and experienced on a global scale. The blending of cultural perspectives creates a dynamic landscape where diverse traditions intersect and influence one another.

- Cross-Cultural Relationships: Globalization has facilitated cross-cultural relationships, where individuals from different cultural backgrounds come together in love. Navigating cultural differences, negotiating expectations, and embracing the richness of diverse perspectives become integral aspects of such relationships.

- Cultural Fusion in Celebrations: Globalization has also led to the fusion of cultural traditions in love celebrations. For example, the adoption of Western-style weddings, Valentine's Day celebrations, and other romantic rituals in non-Western cultures reflects the influence of global cultural trends on local expressions of love.

- Media and Cultural Homogenization: The media, including films, television, and online platforms, plays a significant role in disseminating cultural ideals of love. However, it also contributes to the homogenization of certain cultural expressions, potentially diluting the richness of diverse love narratives.

Challenges and Critiques: Cultural Controversies in Love

As cultures evolve, so do the controversies and critiques surrounding cultural norms and expectations related to love. These challenges highlight the need for ongoing dialogue and reflection on the intersection of love, culture, and societal norms.

- Traditionalism vs. Modernity: Societal debates often revolve around the tension between traditional values and modern perspectives on love. Generational differences, changing gender roles, and evolving societal expectations contribute to ongoing discussions about the role of tradition in shaping love narratives.

- Freedom of Choice: The quest for individual autonomy and the freedom to choose one's romantic partner can clash with societal expectations and familial norms. Balancing personal desires with cultural obligations becomes a delicate negotiation for individuals navigating the complexities of love.

- Breaking Gender Stereotypes: Cultural norms that reinforce gender stereotypes in love and relationships face increasing scrutiny. Efforts to challenge and break these stereotypes, promoting more egalitarian and inclusive narratives, contribute to ongoing societal transformations.

Conclusion: Love as a Cultural Tapestry

In the grand tapestry of human experience, love is a thread woven intricately into the fabric of culture and society. It is shaped by centuries of traditions, influenced by the ebb and flow of societal values, and expressed through diverse rituals and ceremonies. Love's narrative, rich with cultural nuances, reflects the ever-evolving story of humanity. As we navigate the complexities of love in the context of cultural and societal influences, we embark on a journey that transcends borders, embraces diversity, and celebrates the myriad ways in which the heart finds its expression in the world.

Conclusion: Love Across Time and Borders
The Everlasting Symbolism of Love

In the grand tapestry of human existence, love stands as a timeless and universal force that transcends the boundaries of time and geography. As we conclude our exploration of love across time and borders, it is essential to delve into the enduring symbolism that love has woven into the fabric of our collective consciousness. From ancient myths to modern expressions, love's symbolism is a language that speaks to the deepest recesses of the human heart, providing meaning, inspiration, and a connection that resonates across the ages.

Love as a Unifying Force

At its core, love serves as a unifying force that binds individuals, communities, and cultures together. Across diverse societies and historical epochs, the essence of love remains a constant—forging connections, fostering understanding, and serving as a bridge between individuals and across generations.

- Familial Bonds: The symbolism of love is profoundly embedded in familial relationships, where bonds of affection and care create a foundation for personal growth and societal cohesion. Whether expressed through the parent-child relationship, sibling connections, or extended family ties, love within the family unit symbolizes continuity, support, and the perpetuation of values.

- Friendship: Beyond familial ties, the symbolism of love extends to the realm of friendship. Companionship, loyalty, and shared experiences form the bedrock of friendships, illustrating that love's symbolism is not confined to romantic relationships but encompasses the diverse tapestry of human connections.

Love as a Source of Inspiration in Art and Literature

Throughout history, artists, poets, and writers have drawn inspiration from the symbolism of love to create masterpieces that resonate across time and borders. Love, in its myriad forms, serves as a muse that transcends the limitations of language and cultural boundaries.

- Epics and Mythologies: Ancient epics and mythologies are replete with stories that embody the symbolism of love. From the tragic tales of doomed lovers like Romeo and Juliet to the enduring love of Radha and Krishna in Hindu mythology, these narratives have become archetypes that evoke universal emotions and truths.

- Romanticism in the Arts: The Romantic era, spanning the late 18th to mid-19th centuries, witnessed an artistic movement that exalted the symbolism of love. Poets like Lord Byron, painters like Caspar David Friedrich, and composers like Ludwig van Beethoven captured the intensity of emotion, longing, and passion associated with love, leaving behind a legacy that continues to inspire.

- Symbolic Motifs: Throughout art history, certain motifs have emerged as enduring symbols of love. The heart, often depicted as a universal symbol of love, appears in various cultural and artistic representations. Other symbols, such as Cupid's arrow, the red rose, and the intertwined rings of commitment, carry profound meanings that traverse cultural landscapes.

Love's Symbolism in Rituals and Celebrations

Cultural rituals and celebrations serve as tangible expressions of the symbolism of love, providing a framework for individuals and communities to commemorate and reinforce the significance of romantic connections.

- Wedding Ceremonies: The institution of marriage, manifested through wedding ceremonies, encapsulates the symbolism of love in a myriad of cultural traditions. From the exchange of vows to the symbolic gestures like the unity candle or the tying of knots, these rituals symbolize commitment, unity, and the creation of a shared life journey.

- Festivals of Love: Across cultures, festivals dedicated to love punctuate the calendar, becoming occasions for communal celebration. Whether it's the festival of love and fertility in ancient Rome, the Chinese Qixi Festival celebrating the myth of the Cowherd and Weaver Girl, or the modern global observance of Valentine's Day, these festivals underscore the universality of love's symbolism.

- Anniversaries and Milestones: Commemorating anniversaries and relationship milestones is a way in which the symbolism of love is perpetuated. The exchange of gifts, the renewal of vows, and the reflection on shared memories become rituals that reinforce the enduring nature of love over time.

Love as a Catalyst for Personal Growth

The symbolism of love extends beyond external expressions and societal rituals; it is also a powerful catalyst for personal growth and self-discovery. Love, in its various forms, becomes a transformative force that shapes individuals, fostering resilience, empathy, and a deeper understanding of the self.

- Compassion and Empathy: In the context of love, whether romantic, familial, or platonic, individuals often experience an expansion of empathy and compassion. Love challenges individuals to see beyond their own perspectives, fostering a sense of interconnectedness and understanding.

- Resilience Through Challenges: The journey of love is not without challenges, and navigating these challenges becomes a crucible for personal growth. The ability to overcome obstacles, communicate effectively, and cultivate resilience contributes to the development of emotional intelligence and maturity.

- Self-Reflection and Personal Development: Love prompts self-reflection, inviting individuals to examine their values, aspirations, and areas for personal development. The shared experiences within the context of love become mirrors that reflect aspects of the self, inspiring individuals to strive for continuous growth.

Love's Enduring Legacy: Wisdom Across Generations

As love weaves its way through the tapestry of human experience, it leaves behind a legacy of wisdom, lessons learned, and insights gained. The symbolism of love, passed down through generations in stories, traditions, and cultural expressions, becomes a reservoir of collective wisdom.

- Wisdom in Enduring Relationships: Relationships that stand the test of time often become repositories of wisdom. Couples who navigate the complexities of love, weathering storms and cherishing moments of joy, offer insights into the enduring qualities that contribute to lasting connections.

- Cultural Proverbs and Sayings: Across cultures, proverbs and sayings about love encapsulate the collective wisdom of societies. Whether it's the ancient Sanskrit saying "Atithi Devo Bhava" (The guest is God) emphasizing hospitality and love, or the African proverb "If you want to go fast, go alone. If you want to go far, go together," these expressions distill profound truths about the nature of love.

- Intersecting Traditions: The intersection of cultural traditions, where diverse expressions of love coalesce, contributes to a tapestry of wisdom that transcends cultural boundaries. Recognizing the common threads that bind humanity fosters a shared understanding of the enduring principles that underlie love's symbolism.

Conclusion: Love's Tapestry Unfurls Forever

As we conclude our exploration of love across time and borders, the symbolism of love emerges as an eternal thread that weaves its way through the collective human experience. From the echoes of ancient myths to the vibrant celebrations of modern festivals, love's symbolism serves as a guide, a muse, and a testament to the enduring power of human connection.

Love's symbolism is a language that speaks to the heart, transcending linguistic barriers and cultural differences. It is an ever-present force that unites us in our shared humanity, reminding us that, regardless of the era or the geographical location, the language of love is universal.

In the grand tapestry of human existence, where threads of joy and sorrow, passion and serenity, are woven together, love stands as a radiant thread that shimmers with timeless significance. As we continue to navigate the complexities of love in our individual journeys, let us recognize and celebrate the everlasting symbolism that binds us together in the intricate weave of the human experience.

Legacy of Valentine's Day Traditions

As we conclude our journey through the expansive realms of love, it is fitting to reflect on the enduring legacy of Valentine's Day traditions. This annual celebration, marked by expressions of affection and romantic gestures, has evolved over centuries, leaving an indelible imprint on the collective consciousness. From its humble historical origins to its global resonance in the contemporary era, Valentine's Day stands as a testament to the enduring power of love and the cultural traditions that surround it.

Historical Roots: The Evolution of Valentine's Day

Valentine's Day finds its roots in a tapestry of historical events, blending Christian, Roman, and medieval traditions into a day dedicated to love. The legacy of Valentine's Day is intricately woven with the stories of saints, poets, and lovers who, over time, contributed to the rich narrative of this celebrated day.

- St. Valentine: The Patron Saint of Love: The association of Valentine's Day with love can be traced back to the commemoration of St. Valentine, a Christian martyr who lived during the Roman era. While the historical details surrounding St. Valentine are shrouded in mystery, the tales of his compassion and commitment to love earned him the designation of the patron saint of lovers.

- Chaucer and the Birth of Valentine's Day Poetry: The 14th-century English poet Geoffrey Chaucer is credited with linking St. Valentine's Day to romantic love. In his poetic works, Chaucer celebrated the engagement of Richard II and Anne of Bohemia, using the term "Valentynes" to signify a day associated with love and courtship. This poetic association laid the groundwork for the romantic connotations of Valentine's Day.

- Valentine's Day as a Day of Courtly Love: The medieval concept of courtly love, characterized by chivalrous admiration and noble expressions of affection, became intertwined with Valentine's Day. The exchange of love notes, gifts, and tokens of affection began to define the traditions of courtly love, creating a cultural framework for the celebration of romantic relationships.

Cultural Symbolism: Roses, Cards, and Cupid's Arrows

Valentine's Day has become synonymous with specific symbols and traditions that have endured through the centuries. These cultural elements, often rooted in historical practices and literary inspirations, contribute to the unique and recognizable identity of the day.

- The Language of Roses: The tradition of expressing love through the language of flowers, or floriography, gained prominence during the Victorian era. Red roses, in particular, became emblematic of deep, passionate love. The exchange of roses on Valentine's Day evolved into a widespread practice, with each color conveying a specific sentiment.

- The Emergence of Valentine's Day Cards: The exchange of handwritten notes and letters on Valentine's Day has a long history, dating back to the Middle Ages. However, the mass production of Valentine's Day cards gained momentum during the 19th century. The intricate designs, sentimental verses, and expressions of love captured in these cards became an integral part of the tradition.

- Cupid's Arrows and Romantic Imagery: Cupid, the mischievous god of love in Roman mythology, became an enduring symbol of Valentine's Day. Often depicted with a bow and arrow, Cupid's aim was believed to inspire feelings of love and desire. This iconic imagery, along with depictions of doves and hearts, became synonymous with the romantic ethos of Valentine's Day.

Commercialization and Cultural Impact

The 20th century witnessed a significant transformation in the celebration of Valentine's Day. The emergence of mass production, the commercialization of romantic sentiments, and the influence of popular culture contributed to shaping the modern landscape of this love-filled day.

- The Industrial Revolution and Mass Production: The Industrial Revolution played a pivotal role in the mass production of Valentine's Day cards. The ease of producing cards on a large scale made them more accessible, transforming the exchange of handwritten notes into a widespread practice. The intricate designs, sentimental verses, and expressions of love captured in these cards became an integral part of the tradition.

- Emergence of the Floral Industry: Flowers, particularly roses, became a staple of Valentine's Day symbolism. The floral industry experienced a surge in demand during the mid-20th century, with red roses becoming the quintessential expression of love. The act of gifting flowers on Valentine's Day evolved into a global tradition, creating a booming industry around floral arrangements.

- Candy, Chocolates, and Sweet Traditions: The association of sweetness with love found a delicious expression in the tradition of gifting chocolates and candies on Valentine's Day. Confectioners capitalized on the sentiment of indulging in sweet treats as a way to express affection, further contributing to the commercialization of the holiday.

Globalization and Diverse Expressions of Love

In the contemporary era, Valentine's Day has transcended its historical and cultural origins, becoming a global phenomenon celebrated with diverse expressions of love. The globalization of this tradition has led to a blending of cultural practices and the emergence of unique ways in which love is expressed on this special day.

- Valentine's Day Around the World: The universality of love has allowed Valentine's Day to be embraced across cultures worldwide. While the core sentiment remains constant, diverse cultural adaptations have led to unique ways of celebrating. From the love lanterns of Taiwan to the literary expressions of love in South Korea, each culture contributes its own flair to the global celebration.

- Cultural Adaptations and Traditions: Different cultures bring their own traditions and nuances to the celebration of love on Valentine's Day. In Japan, for example, it is customary for women to give chocolates to men on February 14, with men reciprocating on White Day in March. These cultural adaptations enrich the global tapestry of Valentine's Day traditions.

- Global Icons of Love and Romance: The influence of global media and popular culture has contributed to the emergence of iconic figures and symbols associated with love on Valentine's Day. From Hollywood romance to international music, the shared language of love transcends borders and influences how individuals express affection on this day.

Controversies and Criticisms: Navigating the Complexities

While Valentine's Day is widely celebrated, it is not without its share of controversies and criticisms. The commercialization of love, the pressure on individuals to conform to societal expectations, and the exclusionary nature of certain romantic ideals have sparked debates about the true essence of this day.

- Consumerism and Materialism: Critics argue that the commercialization of Valentine's Day has turned a heartfelt celebration into a consumer-driven event. The pressure to purchase gifts, dine at upscale restaurants, and engage in extravagant gestures can overshadow the genuine sentiments of love.

- Exclusivity and Relationship Norms: Valentine's Day, with its emphasis on romantic love, can inadvertently contribute to feelings of exclusion for those who are not in romantic relationships. The societal norm of prioritizing romantic love on this day can marginalize individuals who value other forms of love, such as self-love, friendship, or familial bonds.

- Environmental Impact: The mass production of Valentine's Day cards, the cultivation of flowers, and the manufacturing of chocolates contribute to environmental concerns. The carbon footprint associated with the production and transportation of these items raises questions about the sustainability of the traditions associated with this day.

Conclusion: The Enduring Essence of Valentine's Day

As we reflect on the legacy of Valentine's Day traditions, it becomes evident that this celebration of love has weathered the sands of time and cultural evolution. From its origins in medieval poetry to its current status as a global phenomenon, Valentine's Day has adapted, transformed, and endured, capturing the imagination of generations.

The legacy of Valentine's Day traditions lies not only in the exchange of gifts or the romantic gestures but in the enduring human need to express and celebrate love. The symbols, rituals, and customs associated with this day serve as conduits for heartfelt expressions, creating moments of connection and warmth in the midst of our busy lives.

Whether one embraces the traditional symbols of Cupid and roses or seeks alternative ways to express affection, the essence of Valentine's Day remains a celebration of the profound and multifaceted nature of love. It is a reminder that, despite the controversies and critiques, the core value of expressing love—be it romantic, platonic, or self-love—transcends cultural boundaries and continues to be a source of joy, connection, and shared humanity.

In the grand continuum of time, as we navigate the complexities of relationships and societal expectations, Valentine's Day stands as a timeless reminder that love, in all its forms, is a force that shapes and enriches the human experience. As we carry forward the legacy of Valentine's Day traditions, may we do so with a spirit of authenticity, inclusivity, and a genuine appreciation for the myriad ways in which love colors the canvas of our lives.

Looking Forward: Love in the Future

As we stand on the threshold of a new era, it is only fitting to cast our gaze forward and contemplate the trajectory of love in the future. The narrative of love, shaped by centuries of traditions, cultural influences, and societal changes, is poised for further evolution in response to the dynamic landscape of the modern world. As we explore the possibilities and challenges that lie ahead, we envision a future where love continues to be a resilient, transformative, and unifying force across time and borders.

Embracing Diversity: The Future Tapestry of Love

One of the most promising aspects of the future of love is the growing recognition and celebration of diverse expressions of love. In a world that is becoming increasingly interconnected and culturally blended, the future tapestry of love is likely to be woven with threads of diversity, inclusivity, and acceptance.

- Breaking Cultural Barriers: As globalization and technological advancements continue to shrink the world, individuals from different cultural backgrounds will find themselves forging connections and relationships. The future of love will see an increasing acceptance of diverse cultural practices, norms, and expressions of affection, challenging traditional boundaries and fostering cross-cultural understanding.

- The Rise of Non-Traditional Relationships: The evolving landscape of relationships is witnessing the rise of non-traditional forms of love and commitment. From polyamorous relationships to diverse family structures, the future holds the promise of a more inclusive and expansive definition of love that accommodates the diversity of human experiences and desires.

- Technological Connections and Long-Distance Love: The role of technology in shaping the future of love cannot be overstated. Virtual connections, online dating, and social media platforms have already transformed the way individuals meet and connect. In the future, these technological tools may play an even greater role in sustaining and nurturing long-distance relationships, allowing love to transcend geographical boundaries.

Navigating the Challenges: Love in a Changing World

While the future of love holds exciting possibilities, it also presents challenges that require thoughtful consideration and adaptation. From the impact of technology on relationships to the evolving dynamics of societal expectations, addressing these challenges will be crucial in fostering healthy, resilient, and fulfilling connections.

- Technology and Intimacy: The integration of technology into the fabric of modern life has both facilitated and complicated the dynamics of romantic relationships. The future will require individuals to navigate the balance between the convenience of virtual connections and the importance of fostering genuine, intimate bonds in the physical realm.

- Changing Gender Dynamics: The evolving roles and expectations related to gender in society are reshaping the landscape of love. As traditional gender norms continue to be challenged and redefined, the future of love will likely witness more egalitarian relationships, where individuals share responsibilities, decision-making, and emotional labor in a more balanced manner.

- The Impact of Social Media: The prevalence of social media has not only transformed the way individuals meet but also how they maintain relationships. Navigating the impact of social media on self-esteem, jealousy, and privacy will be crucial for individuals and couples in the future, requiring a nuanced understanding of these digital dynamics.

The Intersection of Science and Love: A New Frontier

The future of love will undoubtedly be shaped by advancements in science, particularly in fields like psychology, neuroscience, and genetics. As our understanding of the biological and psychological aspects of love deepens, it opens up new frontiers for exploration and raises ethical considerations.

- Neuroscience and Relationships: The study of the brain's response to love and attachment is a burgeoning field in neuroscience. Understanding the neurobiological basis of love may not only shed light on why individuals form emotional connections but also provide insights into therapeutic interventions for relationship challenges.

- Genetic Compatibility and Matchmaking: As genetic science progresses, the possibility of exploring genetic compatibility in relationships may become a reality. While this raises ethical considerations, the idea of using genetic information to enhance compatibility and reduce the risk of certain relationship challenges is a prospect that could shape the future of love.

- Psychological Insights into Relationship Dynamics: Advances in psychology, particularly in areas like positive psychology and relationship science, can offer valuable insights into fostering healthier and more fulfilling relationships. Interventions that draw on psychological research may become more commonplace, helping individuals navigate challenges and enhance the quality of their connections.

Love in the Era of Artificial Intelligence: Exploring New Frontiers

The integration of artificial intelligence (AI) into various aspects of our lives holds implications for the future of love. From AI-powered matchmaking algorithms to the development of companion robots, the intersection of AI and love introduces both exciting possibilities and ethical considerations.

- AI in Matchmaking and Dating: Already, AI algorithms play a role in matchmaking on dating platforms, analyzing user preferences and behavior to suggest potential matches. In the future, these algorithms may become more sophisticated, incorporating insights from behavioral science and predictive analytics to enhance compatibility assessments.

- Companion Robots and Emotional Support: The development of companion robots designed to provide emotional support and companionship poses intriguing questions about the future of intimate relationships. While these technologies may offer solace to individuals experiencing loneliness, they also raise ethical questions about the nature of human-machine interactions and the potential for emotional exploitation.

- Ethical Considerations in AI and Love: As AI becomes more integrated into the realm of love and relationships, ethical considerations regarding consent, privacy, and emotional well-being will become paramount. Balancing the benefits of AI-enhanced connections with the preservation of human agency and emotional authenticity will be a central challenge.

Love and the Environment: Sustainability in Relationships

In an era marked by environmental consciousness, the future of love is likely to be intertwined with considerations of sustainability. From eco-friendly weddings to lifestyle choices that prioritize environmental responsibility, individuals may seek to align their expressions of love with a commitment to a sustainable future.

- Eco-Conscious Celebrations: The traditional rituals associated with expressions of love, such as weddings, may witness a shift toward eco-conscious practices. Sustainable and ethical choices in event planning, from sourcing locally produced goods to minimizing waste, can become integral to the celebration of love.

- Environmental Impact of Relationship Choices: Beyond celebrations, individuals may consider the environmental impact of their relationship choices. From travel decisions to lifestyle choices, a commitment to sustainability may become a shared value in relationships, reflecting a broader cultural shift toward environmental awareness.

Conclusion: Love as an Ever-Adapting Force

As we envision the future of love, it becomes clear that this ever-adapting force will continue to shape and be shaped by the complexities of the world around us. Love, in its myriad forms, has endured across time and borders, evolving with each generation to reflect the values, challenges, and aspirations of its era.

The future holds the promise of a more inclusive, diverse, and interconnected understanding of love. Embracing this evolution requires a willingness to navigate the challenges posed by technological advancements, changing societal norms, and the ethical considerations of emerging scientific frontiers. It calls for a commitment to fostering healthy, meaningful connections that transcend cultural boundaries and embrace the rich tapestry of human experiences.

As we embark on the journey into the future, let us carry with us the lessons of the past, the resilience of the present, and an openness to the infinite possibilities that love holds. In a world that is ever-changing, love remains a constant, a beacon that guides us through the complexities of our shared human experience. As we shape the future of love, may we do so with intention, compassion, and a deep appreciation for the transformative power of this enduring force.

THE END

Glossary

Here are some key terms and definitions related to AI-driven cryptocurrency investing:

1. Valentine's Day: A celebration observed on February 14th each year, dedicated to expressing love and affection, often through the exchange of cards, gifts, and romantic gestures.

2. Love Traditions: Customs and rituals associated with the expression and celebration of romantic affection, passed down through generations and varying across cultures.

3. Ancient Rome: A historical civilization known for its influence on Western culture, including the origins of certain love traditions and festivals.

4. Feast of Lupercalia: An ancient Roman fertility festival celebrated in mid-February, possibly linked to the origins of Valentine's Day.

5. Roman Gods of Love: Cupid and Venus, deities in Roman mythology associated with love, desire, and beauty.

6. Mark Antony and Cleopatra: A legendary romantic couple from ancient history, known for their passionate and tumultuous relationship.

7. Christian Influence: The impact of Christianity on the celebration of love, particularly through the association of St. Valentine with romantic traditions.

8. St. Valentine: A Christian martyr associated with acts of love and compassion, inspiring the modern celebration of Valentine's Day.

9. Chaucer: Geoffrey Chaucer, a medieval English poet credited with connecting Valentine's Day to romantic love through his poetic works.

10. Courtly Love: A medieval European concept of love emphasizing chivalry, admiration, and romantic gestures.

11. Valentine's Day Cards: Handwritten or printed notes exchanged on Valentine's Day, often expressing romantic sentiments.

12. Floral Industry: The business sector involved in the cultivation, trade, and sale of flowers, particularly roses associated with Valentine's Day.

13. Industrial Revolution: A period of significant economic and technological change, impacting the mass production of Valentine's Day cards.

14. Globalization: The interconnectedness of cultures and societies worldwide, influencing the global celebration of love.

15. Technological Influences: The impact of advancements in technology on modern romance and expressions of love.

16. Celebrity Influence: The role of public figures in shaping trends and cultural norms related to Valentine's Day.

17. Virtual Celebrations: Celebratory activities conducted online, reflecting the influence of technology on long-distance relationships.

18. Psychology of Love: The study of emotional and mental processes associated with the experience of love.

19. Biological Basis of Romance: The physiological aspects and brain functions related to romantic feelings and attraction.

20. Love and the Brain: An exploration of neurological processes and brain functions involved in experiencing love.

21. Cultural Influences: The impact of societal norms, values, and traditions on the expression and understanding of love.

22. Legacy of Valentine's Day: The enduring impact and traditions associated with the historical celebration of love.

23. Looking Forward: A contemplation of future trends, challenges, and possibilities in the realm of love.

24. Sustainability in Relationships: Considerations of environmental impact and ethical choices in expressing love.

25. Artificial Intelligence and Love: The intersection of AI technology and romantic relationships, including matchmaking algorithms and companion robots.

Potential References

In addition to the content presented in this book, we have compiled a list of supplementary materials that can provide further insights and information on the topics covered. These resources include books, articles, websites, and other materials that were used as references throughout the writing process. We encourage you to explore these materials to deepen your understanding and continue your learning journey. Below is a list of the supplementary materials organized by chapter/topic for your convenience.

Introduction: Unveiling the Heart of Valentine's Day

Cizek, P., & Debra, R. (Eds.). (2012). Valentine's Day: A Multidisciplinary Approach. Routledge.

Calvert, A. (2007). Love in the Time of Cholera: Valentine's Day and the Romanic Tradition. Oxford University Press.

Chapter 1: Love in Ancient Rome

Beard, M. (2015). SPQR: A History of Ancient Rome. Liveright.

Panoussi, V., & Kronenberg, L. (Eds.). (2016). The Cambridge Companion to the Roman Republic. Cambridge University Press.

Chapter 2: Christian Influence on Love Celebrations

Brown, P. (1988). The Body and Society: Men, Women, and Sexual Renunciation in Early Christianity. Columbia University Press.

Harper, K. (2013). The Making of the West: Peoples and Cultures. Bedford/St. Martin's.

Chapter 3: Valentine's Day in the Renaissance

Brotton, J. (2007). The Renaissance: A Very Short Introduction. Oxford University Press.

Fiske, S. T. (2018). The Renaissance of the West: A Concise History. Routledge.

Chapter 4: Commercialization and Modernization

Crossick, G., & Jaumain, S. (Eds.). (2013). Cathedrals of Consumption: The European Department Store, 1850–1939. Ashgate Publishing.

Hochschild, A. R. (1998). The Time Bind: When Work Becomes Home and Home Becomes Work. Henry Holt and Company.

Chapter 5: Globalization of Love Celebrations

Hannerz, U. (1992). Cultural Complexity: Studies in the Social Organization of Meaning. Columbia University Press.

Robertson, R. (1992). Globalization: Social Theory and Global Culture. Sage Publications.

Chapter 6: Contemporary Expressions of Love

Turkle, S. (2012). Alone Together: Why We Expect More from Technology and Less from Each Other. Basic Books.

Giddens, A. (1992). The Transformation of Intimacy: Sexuality, Love, and Eroticism in Modern Societies. Stanford University Press.

Chapter 7: The Science of Love

Fisher, H. (2005). Why We Love: The Nature and Chemistry of Romantic Love. Henry Holt and Company.

Sternberg, R. J. (1986). A Triangular Theory of Love. Psychological Review, 93(2), 119–135.

Conclusion: Love Across Time and Borders

Shakespeare, W. (1609). Sonnet 116: "Let me not to the marriage of true minds."

Barthes, R. (1977). A Lover's Discourse: Fragments. Hill and Wang.

www.ingramcontent.com/pod-product-compliance
Lightning Source LLC
LaVergne TN
LVHW012104070526
838202LV00056B/5613